Renewing the Face of the Earth

Essays in Contemporary Church-World Relationships

BY THOMAS P. NEILL

EDITED BY HARRY J. CARGAS

THE BRUCE PUBLISHING COMPANY / *Milwaukee*

NIHIL OBSTAT:

    JOHN A. SCHULIEN, S.T.D.
    Censor librorum

IMPRIMATUR:

    ✠ WILLIAM E. COUSINS
    Archbishop of Milwaukee
    June 24, 1968

Library of Congress Catalog Card Number: 68–55282

Copyright © 1968 THOMAS P. NEILL, PH.D.

MADE IN THE UNITED STATES OF AMERICA

THIS BOOK, WITH ALL OF THE WORK THAT WENT
INTO MAKING IT, IS DEDICATED WITH LOVE TO
JOHN F. NEILL
AND
MARTIN DE PORRES CARGAS
WHO ARE HELPING TO RENEW THE FACE OF THE EARTH

Introduction

The greater part of a generation has elapsed since I was first influenced by the writings of Dr. Thomas P. Neill, professor of history at St. Louis University. His impact began on me when, still an undergraduate, I was assigned to read *Makers of the Modern Mind* in college. Since then I have become familiar with most of Dr. Neill's nearly fifteen books. Some I have had the pleasure of reviewing. Several I read in preparation for a television discussion program on which we both appeared. Most I have taken off the shelves only because I wished to.

For the past six years, I have taken pride in the fact that Tom Neill is a colleague of mine at St. Louis University. Now, his friendship as well as his writings are of value to me. By reputation, Neill might be felt to be the kind of intellectual theoretician who speaks only to those who live in dreamland, who has nothing to say to those of us who live outside the test tube. But Tom Neill is a former college baseball coach and a soccer buff in a community teeming with soccer enthusiasts. These interests symbolize well, I think, his contact with a down to earth reality that this collection of columns from *The St. Louis Review* proves.

In his concern with the real significance of worldly affairs, Thomas Neill is a true Teilhardian.

The title of this work is taken from a remark made by Teilhard de Chardin, who wondered if the biblical quotation, "And Thou shalt renew the face of the earth" might not have some important reference to the evolution in which man participates and in fact helps to create; what Karl Rahner would call Man's "self-manipulation." I am convinced that Neill sees what Teilhard saw: that the world is man in different stages of becoming.

If this is true, of course, then the implications of this on the notion of the Mystical Body are immense. Ultimately, in a less than mysterious way, I am you and you are me. Your good work is important to me just as my sin is important to you. Furthermore, what DeGaulle, Mao, Lyndon Johnson, George Wallace, and other world figures do is of spiritual significance to us all. Not only are their acts of political impact but they bear very much on our membership in the Mystical Body. As the world rushes to union in Christ (Teilhard's Omega Point toward which the evolutionary process is directed) all such men either help to hasten or delay this process.

But Neill is saying more in these columns as well. He is saying that we unknowns who prefer to let the problems of war, integration, poverty, and the like be taken care of by those mentioned above while we watch pro football — that we too have the great obligation to help renew the face of the earth. Gustav Weigel wrote that Teilhard was shouting to the theologians to enlarge their borders. I believe that Tom Neill is shouting the same thing to us.

The importance of man's creative participation in renewing the face of the earth is emphasized by Teilhard in *The Divine Milieu* when, in speaking of the individual man he writes:

> By his fidelity he must *construct* — starting from the most natural zone of his own self — a work, an *opus*, into which something enters from all the elements of the earth. He makes his own soul throughout all his earthly days; and at the same time he collaborates on another work, in another *opus*, which infinitely transcends, while at the same time it narrowly determines, the perspectives of his individual achievement: the completion of the world.

Long prior to the time he read this passage Neill knew it. Again, these *St. Louis Review** pieces are not only his *opus*, but are meant to be a guide for our work as well. Here is the teacher of the highest order: the person whose teachings are also his life.

---

* Here Dr. Neill and I would like to express our gratitude to Donald Quinn and the *St. Louis Review* for permission to reprint Dr. Neill's columns.

There is much more of a parallel with Teilhard's thought in Professor Neill's philosophy than can be presented here. Only a few things can be hinted. For example, Teilhard felt passionately as Sir Julian Huxley noted "that East and West are culturally complementary, and that both are needed for the further synthesis and unification of world thought." With the perspective of the truly experienced historian, Neill points this up in his columns dealing with U. S. Far Eastern policies. I think further that Neill's belief is in agreement with Teilhard's who wrote in his most important work, *The Phenomenon of Man:* "The final convergence will take place in peace."

It might be unfair to Dr. Neill to let the above paragraph go without adding that I am not certain if he is a pacifist, an anti-Johnson Democrat, a Republican, or what have you. On these points his writings need not be explicit. I do know that among his admirers are men who honestly believe in the necessity of American military might as well as dedicated pacifists; Lyndon Johnson supporters and Lyndon Johnson detractors; liberals and conservatives; retired professors and college sophomores.

The reason for this respect is readily observable in the collection which follows. Thomas Neill has written with much insight and with much criticism at times, but always about a world he loves, a nation he loves, a Church he loves. He has the long view and I think this communicates itself very well.

Harry J. Cargas
St. Louis University

Preface

A columnist is occasionally, and properly, asked why he has adopted the position he holds about the church and its place in the modern, changing world. He can answer such questions, I believe, only by telling of his own background. Is he a recent convert to the church? Is he a former seminarian, especially a former Jesuit or other religious seminarian? How did he ever drift into the business of writing a column about church or other affairs every week?

Each columnist's background is unique, his own, and I feel called upon to explain mine, because I feel it is quite different from that of other Catholic columnists who write about the church as though it were something "out there" somewhere. They tell of not knowing any bishops personally, of not being able to speak to them, of great difficulty in arranging an audience even with the pastor. I know these men speak the truth, but their experience is not mine — with the rare exception of one pastor, whose painful stay in my parish was rather short.

I have never felt that bishops are, ex officio, "bad guys" or "good guys." They are like the heads of any business, differing according to digestion and temperament — some dyspeptic and others pleasant, some friendly and others coldly distant. Almost universally they have tended to be conservative, apprehensive of change, just like any manager of a large business. I must believe some of the horror stories told about them, and about pastors, because these stories are told by honest, conscientious men. But I have not been so treated.

I have always felt that I belonged in the church. This is the essential point, which can be developed only by excessive use of the first person pronoun, for which I beg the reader's tolerance this one time. My earliest memories of the church were of living on "Catholic Hill" in a mining town in Colorado, across from the church and the rectory. The pastor was a Dane, whose theology I now recognize as having been far advanced over that of American or Irish-educated priests.

An altar-boy at five (if there were any older Catholic boys they were apparently away in school somewhere), I learned both Latin and the reading of phonetic English from the pastor. I also learned pinochle, poker, and rudimentary chess in his study, and I was told that leftover wine in the cruet should not be poured in the sink or put back in the bottle. Because the pastor had no housekeeper, he frequently ate dinner with us. Much to my mother's consternation, he insisted on meat on Friday, since we enjoyed the privilege of the Spanish grant in southwestern Colorado. He also warned her not to be holier than the church, for this is the sin of pride. Because this wonderful Danish priest had difficulty with the American idiom, he brought sermon outlines to my father to have him put them into language which would not amuse and confuse. Thus, I felt I belonged in the church.

My family moved from this mining town when I was nine. We moved frequently during the next few years before settling permanently in St. Louis. During these years I learned there was no great difference between public and parochial schools. I had good and bad teachers in both. I repeatedly recited the catechism in the parochial schools, but the important thing about parochial schools, as against public, was that they were somehow attached to the church building, and we got assignments to serve (especially funerals and weddings, with their customary "honorariums"). Some teachers in both parochial and public schools were wonderful, charitable women, while others were neurotic, sex-obsessed (nuns worse than lay-women as I remember them). At any rate, both nuns and lay-women generally seemed rather nice ladies who sometimes did not know how to pronounce a word or how to spell another, and had to rely on the answer book for arithmetic problems. There was a measure of intolerance in both kinds of schools, and I am not sure which was worse.

The first bishop I knew rescued me from the punishment of haughty nuns, who sent me home for having dirty knuckles after playing marbles during recess. This same bishop dropped into our home occasionally, always coming by the back door because he preferred a cup of coffee in the kitchen to a formal sitting in the parlor. One naturally felt at home with such an ordinary. There followed a short interlude of living in an Irish Catholic ghetto in south Chicago, which maintained a children's Mass on Sunday at which attendance was taken, and voted overwhelming against Al Smith in 1928. Then we settled in St. Louis.

For me personally the Great Depression was probably a fortunate interlude as I went through Catholic high school and college institutions. We read *Quadragesimo Anno*, talked about the social questions, and became immersed in the "Catholic Revival." I understood that this involved intellectuals, but it was some time before I realized that almost all bishops stayed aloof, and most of them were hostile to such "radicals" as Msgr. John A. Ryan of the NCWC's Social Action Department, and indifferent to the Catholic Association for International Peace. By the time I learned this about our bishops, it was like learning that some of my relatives voted Republican, relatives I could criticize constructively and argue with vehemently, but without rancor or bitterness.

This account of how I have come to think of church problems as I do must conclude with a brief statement about my position for the past twenty-five years. I have taught history and directed graduate work at St. Louis University since 1943. Included among my students have been priests who have risen to positions of authority in the church. I know them as students no more infallible than I, and I feel no hesitancy to label their position ill-taken if I think it is. A few of them were brilliant, some clever, some just plain stupid.

More important, my freedom to teach what I think to be true and to conduct research I consider important has never been challenged. I have always been free to say what I think of Jesuits, popes, and councils — which is a wonderfully moderating influence on one's opinions. I have always been consulted on decisions to be made on matters within my purview at St. Louis University, and I have never been made to feel like an employee in this academic community. I am rather an associate in our academic enterprise. Here too, then, I feel like a member free to criticize and offer suggestions without fear of reprisal.

These autobiographical remarks have been made to explain why I feel qualified to make constructive criticisms of my church without being bitter for having been excluded from counseling it, and for understanding from an inside view the human element in the visible lay, clerical, and episcopal church.

THOMAS P. NEILL

Contents

INTRODUCTION   v

PREFACE   ix

PART I.   RENEWAL IN THE CHURCH

   1. Many Things Are Right With Today's Church   3
   2. Celibacy's Complex History   7
   3. The Celibacy Question, Too Real to Ignore   11
   4. Jansenism: the Perennial Heresy   15
   5. Thoughts on the Communication Gap   19
   6. Bill of Rights for Catholics   23
   7. Canon Law Must Fit All Cultures   27
   8. The Challenge to Authority in the Church   31
   9. Pope John Repudiated the Grand Inquisitor   34
  10. That Ugly Cloud of Anticlericalism   37
  11. NCCC Sought a True Church Cross Section   40

PART II.   THE CHURCH IS YOU

   1. How Much Freedom for Students?   45
   2. Student Power and a University's Function   49
   3. The Intellectual Community Speaks to Itself   52
   4. Why Enfranchise the 18-Year-Olds?   55
   5. League of Women Voters   59

6. Washington Bogeyman Still a Phantom   65
7. Decency Is the Only Guard for Privacy   66
8. Problems of Cities, Integration Are the Same   69
9. Reflections on Riots   73
10. Medicare Is Qualified Success   76

PART III. THE CHURCH IN THE MODERN WORLD

1. Was Pope Pius XII a Progressive?   .   81
2. The Practicality of "Idealism"   85
3. Humanism Joins the Church   89
4. U. S. Bishops and Nationalism   92
5. God Becomes a Slogan in Modern Holy Wars   96
6. The Credibility Gap in Church and State   100
7. Chanceries Should Conduct Their Own Surveys   103
8. Lay Boards Were Inevitable   107
9. It's Time to Revamp the Children's Parish   111
10. If Rome Understood the Difference in Cultures 115
11. Looking Upon Our Mother, the Church   118

PART IV. TOWARD PEACE ON EARTH

1. De Gaulle Over 76, Is Argument for Forced
    Retiring at 75   123
2. Mao Must Accommodate to Survive   127
3. A Lesson From History: The Boer War   130
4. Are We Blundering Into Immoral Imperialism?   134
5. U. S. Feels Frustrated by Vietnam   137
6. Thoughts About Our Asian Policy   140
7. A Hoped-for Direction in Foreign Policy   144

PART I

Renewal in the Church

1. Many Things are Right
With Today's Church

I am taking the calculated risk of being labelled a Pollyanna in sounding a note of optimism about the church today. Sounds of alarm and cries of despondency resound everywhere. With the specifics of many alarms I have no quarrel; with others I do. Many face a crisis of faith; others are scandalized to hear Mass in a language they understand; still others believe that religion is intruding into their social and political life in unwarranted fashion; others complain that so-called renewal really means secularization, abandoning the faith, losing vocations, and driving priests and nuns out of religious life.

There is cause for concern with each of these plaints, but they do not present a balanced view of the church today. Even worse, they are usually followed by a wistful sigh for a return to "normality" when the church lived in tranquillity. I am old enough to have lived in that tranquil church. People were generally faithful about attending Mass on Sunday and receiving the Sacraments. Only a handful attended Mass on weekdays. Religious people, especially women, also had their favorite novenas, and many said the rosary every day.

These are good things, of course, but let us remember that they were the totality of religion for most people in the age of tranquillity. What one said about his neighbor or did to his employees or business associates had no relationship to the hour of religion he performed once a week on command and under threat of eternal damnation.

On the surface, the water on which the Ship of Church

floated (the metaphor used twenty years ago) was tranquil. What about under the surface? I remember priests marrying and disappearing. Few knew of such defections because neither secular nor diocesan papers mentioned such things, and those of us who knew pretended it hadn't happened. The leader of a local Communist Party had attended a Catholic university, and he had become a Communist because in his confused way he had identified the church with the exploiting class and accused it of ignoring the poor — with partial justification.

This was the church of tranquillity in which there were no scandals, no crises of belief, no public discussion of religion in the press, and hardly ever even private discussion in living rooms. Religion simply was not interesting enough to make the press or be talked about. And one who raised an issue or questioned a practice was likely to have his holy water cut off. This was the church of tranquillity, the church of apathy. The only action was far away in the missions, which the faithful supported generously.

The winds began to stir, surface waters on the sea of tranquillity began to ripple, and the ship began to move (now let us drop that metaphor forever more). College students began to stay awake in theology (formerly religion) classes, which became challenging and exciting. Feature articles about the Catholic church began to appear in the secular news media. Events in the local churches became newsworthy in the secular press. Many more people read books on religious subjects. Religion became an even hotter discussion topic than sports, politics, and children. More men, women, and children attended Mass on weekdays.

A new vision unfolded, a new vision of the church, the world, our neighbors, ourselves. The vision was disturbing, and to many it was shocking, for we had thought the world was the devil's and we pretended our neighbor did not exist.

The new theologians were confusing us by saying religion was not a simple I-God relationship. We were told that we should find Christ in our neighbor, which is certainly not the Christ we had known. We were told — we who went to Mass on Sunday — that we were somehow responsible for other people's sins. We were told that the anthropomorphic God we had pictured, and most of us saw in religion picture-books in school, was not really a great big Man, that evolution was not necessarily untrue, that the church had made mistakes in the past, that holy orders did not infuse knowledge, and many other shocking things.

This was upsetting. Many asked: "What will they destroy next?" Others complained, "This is not my church." Not many remembered that Christ was a revolutionary figure, that He confused and puzzled His followers, and that the church revolutionized the society in which it dwelled.

Unfortunately, the very nature of the news caused us to overlook many healthy developments in the renewing church. We are preconditioned to dwell on the scandalous and only glance at the rest, and what many consider scandalous is only different from the old ways. Nuns came out of the cloister to work with the poor, the crippled, the downtrodden, and they scandalized us because they did not do it when we were children. For a layman to criticize a priest or a bishop just was not done. That the church is said not to be the monolith we thought it was, demanding conformity in every detail and enforcing it with absolute, arbitrary authority, should not be a cause of scandal just because in the past "ours was not to reason why."

Behind many of these complaints, I suspect, is a hidden pride, the unstated belief that our concept of the church and the world was absolutely right for all time, and any deviation from it must be wrong. We should, I maintain, regain our intellectual and emotional balance by also examining healthy developments. The involvement of lay people in the life of their church is the most obvious of these, and most of all the responsible freedom and the initiative that more and more laymen have begun to exercise.

Two notable examples of this occurred recently in the Midwest. After months of study and planning some laymen of Oklahoma City petitioned Bishop Reed for permission to form an experimental parish without a church building, rectory, or school. They gather for Mass, discussion, and business for three hours every Sunday, and in the words of one of them: "I look forward to Sunday all week long." Remember how long forty-five minutes on Sunday used to be? The other example of lay initiative is in Kansas City, where teachers responsibly worked out a simplified, short Mass for young children. Bishop Helmsing encouraged them and expressed his hope that the American bishops and Rome will give permission for such a Mass.

There are countless other instances throughout the country that give cause for a qualified optimism about the future. One who has never doubted or questioned has never understood. One who has never stumbled has never moved. One who wants absolute conformity in all things does not understand the humanity of Christ or the richness of variety. I, for one, do not want to go back to a church of tranquillity, which has improperly been made synonymous with apathy, or stagnation.

2. Celibacy's Complex History

At their Chicago meeting in 1967, the bishops strongly re-affirmed the church's position on clerical celibacy, but they accepted it as one of the subjects for in-depth study of the priestly life. There is no theological or scriptural problem about a married clergy. The problems are rather how marriage would affect the priest's spiritual life and his ministry, and how a married clergy would be accepted by the people.

It is helpful to see why and how clerical celibacy arose and was perpetuated in the Western Church. The church always held, with St. Paul, that virginity is a higher state, so that those who could live celibately were counseled to do so. There was even more stress on the counsel for poverty. Why the counsel for celibacy became a command and that on poverty grew ever fainter is a complicated story that can only be sketched here.

Originally priests and bishops were chosen from the Christian community, and most of them were married men. Married bishops are found only infrequently in both the Eastern and Western churches after the fifth century, but there was no general law that they be celibate; as late as 867 a married man, Hadrian II, was chosen pope. Celibacy was made a requirement for priests locally, first in Spain and then in other places, until finally the Second Lateran Council ruled in 1139 that no priest in the Roman Rite could contract a valid marriage.

Four interrelated developments in the first five centuries made celibacy a condition for priesthood in the West. These were the sacralization of the priest, a carryover from the Jewish purification rites; the extremist view that intercourse is evil; a perfervid desire to suffer for Christ; and finally the transfer of monastic celibacy to the secular clergy.

At first bishops and priests lived among the people, apparently holding a job like anyone else. They preached, presided at the sacred banquet, and performed the other sacerdotal functions. For centuries they were chosen on the grounds St. Paul gave Timothy: men of learning, good repute, with only one wife, in control of their own households. They lived in the world. As late as 428 Pope Celestine wrote the bishop of Provence to condemn the wearing of distinctive garb (apparently monkish) by his clergy.

In the fourth century more and more writers in both the West and the East began to transfer the sacral nature of the Eucharist to the person of the priest. The Eucharistic celebration was gradually taken from the home into church buildings, in imitation of Jewish and pagan temples, and the priest was set apart from the community as a sacral person. Such a person should not defile himself by sexual relations. At first, writers like Eusebius did not condemn marriage for the clergy, but held that married men should refrain from intercourse with their wives after they became priests because such carnal action was defiling.

Closely related to the sacralization of the priest was the heretical idea that sexual intercourse is essentially evil. This concept came to be widely adopted in modified form in the tradition of the Judeo-Christians and those infected by Manichean thought. Thus prominent authors, such as St. Jerome, St. Ambrose, and St. Augustine, held that married priests should no longer have intercourse with their wives, for this was unworthy of one in the ministry.

Third, Christians in the first five or six centuries were consumed by a zeal to suffer heroically as Christ had suffered for them. Such desire was realized in extreme practices like seeking martyrdom or living a solitary life in the desert. Refraining from sexual intercourse became another and more widely adopted deprivation for those who would be holy persons.

The most important trend in the adoption of clerical celibacy, however, was the transfer of monastic celibacy to the diocesan clergy, especially in the Western church. From the beginning men who retired to the desert or lived in monastic communities were celibates. They excited the admiration of Christians, and there was a natural inclination to adopt as much of their way of life as possible, more in the West than in the East, perhaps because of St. Benedict's moderate rule and the tremendous influence of St. Augustine. At any rate, bishops like St. Ambrose and St. Augustine gathered their clergy to live a community life in the episcopal residence. Such clergy, of course, lived in celibacy.

The result of these four developments was that clerical celibacy became not only the better but the required life in many areas under Roman jurisdiction. Various local synods, beginning early in the fourth century in Spain, made celibacy mandatory. In villages and rural areas, however, a married clergy was not only permitted but was the normal way of life. Priests in these areas could not live in a community of their fellows, and there was no scandal about their being family men.

Thus the celibate state came to be established as the better life when possible. It was consolidated in the Western church, however, for different reasons, for the original causes for this becoming mandatory instead of advisable seem to have practically disappeared.

As feudalism developed in the Middle Ages, each bishop and priest became the holder of a benefice, or income, bestowed by ecclesiastical or lay lords. Benefices were customarily hereditary, and both the Eastern and Western churches did not allow married men to become bishops because the office would normally devolve upon their oldest sons.

This concern was extended to priests as well in the Western church. Documents indicate that the major concern was for priests not to contract marriage so that they would not have legitimate children. There seemed to be relatively little concern by this time that they had concubines, because the children of such relationships were ineligible to inherit the benefice. Considerable revenue in at least some dioceses came from permissions to rural and village priests to have concubines. Thus the con-

cern shifted from the idea that the sacred person, the priest,
should not engage in sexual relations to the concern that his
offspring should not be legitimate.

This explains why the Council of Trent treated the subject of
clerical celibacy in the chapter on matrimony, denying priests'
children the right to church benefices. Clerical concubinage had
become so widespread before Trent that the requirement of celibacy might well have been dropped if the church had not
frozen its position against Luther and other Protestants who
favored a married clergy. Thus Trent kept clerical celibacy without discussion, adverting to it only by spelling out that their
children were not eligible to hold benefices. The Eastern church,
meanwhile, had broken from Rome before clerical celibacy was
made mandatory in 1139 for all priests under Roman jurisdiction.

An historical perspective is helpful, I think, in understanding
how and why the Western church turned the counsel of celibacy
into a mandatory condition for the priesthood, how the removal
of the priest from the world is now repudiated, how the degrada-
tion of sex was derived from pre-Christian thought later condemned, and how feudalism and reaction to Protestantism fixed
the thinking of Rome on this subject.

These historical considerations will undoubtedly be part of
the in-depth study by the American bishops' commission on the
priestly life.

3. The Celibacy Question, Too Real to Ignore

The question of optional celibacy for diocesan clergy has become a recognized concern for the American Catholic Church. Father Fichter's survey showed that a sizeable number of respondents thought priests should have some kind of option between celibacy and the married state, many of them not because they would marry but because of their concern for fellow priests and their effective ministry in the church.

This may not be the most crucial question facing the church today, as some claim, but it is one of the most important, complex and urgent problems now confronting both the American bishops and the faithful, as well as priests. Critics of the Fichter survey do not make the problem go away; at most, if they are sound criticisms, they change the number of priests who believe the problem exists. Certainly compulsory celibacy is one cause for the decline in numbers of young men entering the seminary, and for the increased number of "drop-outs" before and after ordination.

By its very nature the question of optional celibacy is charged with emotionalism, and it easily lends itself to something like a second-rate-movie sensationalism. This is unfortunate, because it prevents serious, objective, scholarly study and discussion of the problem. But the problem remains, and it will not go away if scholars and those in authority simply ignore it. Instead of disappearing, it will increase in intensity.

Highly personal and frequently irrelevant arguments for and against optional celibacy have already beclouded the issue and discouraged some competent scholars from discussing it. Many arguments appear regularly in letters-to-the-editor columns of Catholic papers and magazines. These letters for and against optional celibacy might be misleading as to what American Catholics think about the issue, because only those who feel strongly about an issue write a letter to the editor, and more often than not such a letter-writer expresses an inflexible position for or against the issue, be it Communism, the rosary, or optional celibacy.

Too often those who advocate optional celibacy seem to believe that taking a wife is like taking a pill guaranteed to cure a headache and relieve nervous tension. Marriage is not a panacea that brings instant, perfect, and perpetual happiness. Equally wrong is the unjust accusation that any priest who advocates optional celibacy "just wants to get married." Unrealistic, too, is the argument that a married priest would not have time to tend to his ministry. Much of the opposition to optional celibacy, I am convinced, comes from the Jansenist tradition that marriage is something permitted because of human weakness and the means God devised (in a weak moment) for procreation, and priests should be above it.

It would be good if a moratorium could be enforced on these arguments which mislead, so that the problem can be studied and discussed by scholars to throw light on the subject from their various disciplines: theologians, philosophers, canon lawyers, historians, and especially psychologists and sociologists.

The long-standing law in the Latin Rite requiring celibacy as a condition for the active ministry has caused many American Catholics to confuse vocation to the ministry and the charismatic gift of celibacy. Sound thinking about the problem of optional celibacy must start by distinguishing these two calls. Not all laymen have a vocation to married life, and many of them are judicious enough to realize this.

Compulsory celibacy is not required by theology. The Roman church existed for centuries before celibacy was made compulsory for diocesan priests, and even now exceptions are occasionally made. Nor does Scripture require celibacy as a condition for ordination and service as one of Christ's ministers. Celibacy is required by canon law, of course, and is the distinguishing hallmark of the clergy. The canon requiring celibacy was adopted for good reasons centuries ago, and the key question now is whether present conditions continue to require it.

Thus the immediate areas of investigation are sociological and psychological. It does not suffice for those who oppose optional celibacy to say "America is not ready for it yet," or "the faithful will not respect married priests." No one really knows. That is why thorough, scholarly study must be done by clerical and lay scholars. Meanwhile, theologians and biblical scholars can well explore more deeply the theological and scriptural implications of celibacy, virginity (not a synonym for celibacy), and the married state.

The most telling argument in favor of optional celibacy is that many persons may have a call to the priesthood but not to celibacy. Should such a person be denied the opportunity to follow his vocation? It is hardly in keeping with the spirit of Vatican II to tell him to become an Eastern Rite priest, to turn his back on the culture in which he was raised and on the friends and land he loves. Study may prove that the people of God in the Latin Rite are still unwilling to accept married priests. In that case those who have a vocation to the ministry will simply have to look for a "second-best" vocation, and the church will be less well served. Thus we come around full circle to the very practical consideration that as the church continues to need ever more priests, vocations decline and the People of God are less well served.

One group of theologians, biblical scholars, canon lawyers, and priests with pastoral experience, advocate a study of the problem by the U. S. bishops. They do not denigrate celibacy, nor do they hold that the married state is the better way. Their stand is summed up in these words: "The proposal of optional celibacy is in harmony with the council's emphasis on flexibility and adaptation in promoting pastoral renewal; it also manifests a deep respect for the integrity of the vocations to priesthood, virginity, and marriage, reaffirmed by the Council and recognized as well in the Eastern Rites and in other Christian traditions."

Discussion of this problem is valueless if it is not based on scholarly study. As our pastors and leaders, I think, the American bishops would do well to have a committee of qualified scholars study all aspects of optional celibacy, even to seeing whether there are places where it might be introduced experimentally and on a limited scale. Ignoring the problem will not make it disappear.

4. Jansenism: the Perennial Heresy

The trauma which many of us suffer as a result of changes in the church is due in large part to the Jansenistic legacy with which we live. This distortion of Christianity causes many to be scandalized by true Christianity. Jansenism, or puritanism in the modern Catholic Church, is an expression or an attitude that is older than Christianity. It is one way of man's accounting for the existence of evil in the world and is an endemic reaction of proud people to the fact of fallen human nature. It stands in stark contrast to Christian humanism evidenced in the documents of Vatican II and even more pointedly in Paul VI's *Populorum Progressio*.

Tertullian personified this view early in church history when he expressed Manichean views on the wickedness of the flesh and showed contempt for secular wisdom. His terse "What does Jerusalem have to do with Athens?" remains a classic expression of this anti-humanistic attitude. The more central theme of Christian teaching was developed by Tertullian's contemporary, Origen, who believed that Christianity should incorporate the learning of Athens for the perfection of men in the temporal order.

The Manichean strain was put into the mainstream of Christianity by St. Augustine in the early fifth century, partly as an overreaction to his early sexual misconduct. St. Augustine was the most influential Father of the Western church throughout the Middle Ages, and unfortunately woven into his brilliant dogmatic treatises was the strain of revulsion against the body, sex, and the material world.

This Manichean view was sharpened and updated in the early modern church in the contest between Jesuits and Jansenists. The

Jesuits emphasized man's free response to grace in achieving salvation, and they promoted education in the classical humanities. Jansenists believed that Jesuits were a poisonous body in the church that they were called upon by God to exorcize. Parts of their doctrine and much of their attitude toward life was sharpened in their attacks upon the Jesuits.

Jansenism gets its name from Bishop Cornelius Jansen of Ypres, whose *Augustinus* was supposedly based on the writings of St. Augustine. Jansenists said that Christ did not die for all mankind, but only for the chosen few He has predestined for salvation. They took an unduly optimistic view of man before the fall and an unduly pessimistic view of man after the fall. Free will is nothing but concupiscence, and in his fallen state man can do nothing but sin. The chosen few can no more resist grace than the reprobate can save themselves. Jansenists held that the sacrament of Penance is valid only with perfect contrition, and that no one is worthy to receive Christ in Holy Communion. This sacrament should therefore be received only a few times in a lifetime even by those predestined for salvation, for respectful abstention from communion honors Christ more than frequent reception.

Propositions such as the above were extracted from Jansen's book and condemned by the Holy See, and similar action was taken against writings of later Jansenists. Then began the game of casuistry, with Jansenists accepting the condemnations but maintaining that Jansen and his followers did not mean their statements in the sense in which they were condemned. Philip Hughes observes of Jansenism: "The history of the heresy is a history of endless condemnations, of submissions, of subterfuges by which the heretic when condemned submits and then explains away the submission, is recondemned, submits again, appeals, and submits, and always with a fresh reservation, some new loophole through which he escapes to restate — still within the church — his condemned theory."

At first, some influential families and bishops in the Low Countries and France adopted Jansenism, in whole or in part, as "pure Christianity." They appeared austere, noble people trying to cleanse Christianity from its human weaknesses. Jansenism, like puritanism in Protestant denominations, rubbed off on others, so that large groups who never heard of the original condemned doctrines found themselves accepting certain Jansenistic practices and attitudes. As Jansenism spread, its adherents tended to abandon the original doctrinal position of Jansenism and to concentrate on its negative moral positions.

Sex became an inherent evil not to be discussed. Priests were superior not because they were called to the ministry and received the sacrament of Holy Orders, but because they were strong enough to remain celibate for life. The world was essentially evil; it was to be shunned as much as possible. Religion was severe and essentially negative.

This strain of Jansenism entered this country chiefly through the Irish clergy who were the bishops and pastors almost everywhere until recently. Many of the French clergy who came to this country and Canada were even more Jansenistic, but of course not nearly so numerous as Irishmen. Protestant puritanism affected American Catholics perhaps even more than Catholic Jansenists, but the influx of Catholic Jansenists seemed to give official endorsement to puritan attitudes and morals. Thus a thinned out dye of Jansenism spread among us and remains with many of us today.

A crisis of belief is presently suffered by relatively few in this country, because it is morals rather than dogmas that concern most Americans. This attitude toward moral questions, which is a curious mixture of sound instinct and unsound moral theology, is the visible legacy of Jansenism.

The invisible legacy, like the part of the iceberg under the surface, is the larger and more serious heritage of this heresy. It is the hidden pride of the self-righteous, the complete lack of charity in judging those who are "weak," who now eat meat on Friday, who enjoy singing in church, even off-key. It is the association of real religion with austerity, severity, well-pressed clothes, neatly combed hair, dead silence and a sour face in the awesome presence of God.

It is unfortunate that this aberration is looked upon as the only proper attitude toward forms of worship and ways of living. It is unfortunate because so much of Vatican II's decrees are suspect to such people who believe that the church is compromising with truth and betraying Christ by watering down the message. What but the hidden pride inherent in Jansenism can support such "holiness"?

5. Thoughts on the Communication Gap

Most difficulties in the church, in government, in universities, and in business are put down to "lack of adequate communication." Negotiators between management and labor speak of inadequate communications; the sad plight of some ghettos is blamed partly on failure of communications between those in the ghetto and the rest of the community; the difficulty at St. John's University was largely caused by failure of communications between the administration and the faculty; some 90 percent of priests answering Father Fichter's recent survey of their attitudes felt that they could not readily communicate with their bishops.

The solution to all these difficulties seems to be to establish or open channels of communication. This is necessary, of course, but I submit that this is only a preliminary step in establishing genuine communication. The reaction of some bishops to priests' complaints about lack of communication channels with them indicates the real problem. These bishops say that they inform priests that they are always ready to listen — and I believe many of them really are.

But somehow this statement of willingness does not convince priests, any more than a father's telling his son, "Come talk with me whenever you have a problem." The problem is deeper and more difficult than simply "opening channels of communication."

True, there is a problem of keeping channels of communication open. No bishop, university president, head of a corporation or a bank can be available at all times to their employees. Times must be set, and in most cases secretaries must filter mail, telephone calls, and appointments to protect the "boss" from cranks and other useless communicators. But this problem is resolved by employing competent and discriminating screeners. It is by no means insoluble.

The basic problem of communication is indicated by the fact that almost half the assistant priests answering Father Fichter's survey said that they found communication with the pastor most difficult, if not impossible, and I have been told by older priests that it used to be even worse. There are pastors, for example, who eat alone, live alone in their suites in the rectory, and communicate with their assistants through notes left in a designated place.

I can't think of any better channel of communication than living under the same roof, except perhaps sleeping in the same bed. But marriage counselors tell us that the major factor in most marriage breakdowns is failure of husband and wife to communicate with each other.

The communication problem would be at least partly solved if a true person-to-person dialogue were established rather than a superior-to-inferior conversation. John XXIII, as an example, was able to converse with Vatican gardeners on a person-to-person level, as he could talk with princes and presidents in the same way. This is the mark of a great man, and it shows a sincere desire to listen to the person on the other end of the dialogue. But the person who occupies the inferior position socially or legally also bears some share of blame in failing to communicate.

The priest who does obtain "an audience" with his bishop, or the instructor who does get an appointment to speak with the dean, must have the courage to say what he believes and presume that the correspondent in the dialogue is willing to listen and to modify his position on receipt of new information.

The problem seems to resolve itself into a feeling of insecurity on the part of both persons. I know a janitor — but only one — who philosophically shares his thoughts with me, and (I hope) I with him. We feel we are equals on the level of our discussion.

But other janitors, and most students, are afraid that if they really try to speak their thoughts to me they will sound foolish.

Some people are incapable of engaging in effective communication. They are not able to express their real ideas and feelings. We will always have a number of such husbands and wives, bishops and priests, employers and employees, fathers and sons, mothers and daughters.

This is a psychological and sometimes psychiatric difficulty that no "opening of channels of communication" can resolve. Despite what John Donne said, such people remain "islands."

I do not believe, however, that the difficulty to express oneself is nearly as general as the difficulty of listening, of conceding that perhaps others might have something to say that deserves attention.

There are the classic examples of "suggestion boxes" that the employer empties periodically without reading the notes, and of bishops who have periodic "open hours" during which they sit behind their desks and listen smilingly to anything said, but proceed when the time is over as though nothing had been said. There are examples all of us have seen of several people listening intently to each other — but only for the second of silence in order to get his own story told. These are instances of absolute failure of communication where channels could not be better established.

It is strange indeed that every school and college has many courses in effective speaking, but I have never found one with a course in effective listening. It is a fact, though, that a telephone has two termini, and effective speaking is wasted unless there is also effective listening.

A given percentage of college students can always be counted on not to have heard an assignment properly or read an examination question accurately. And there is the old experiment of whispering a simple statement into a person's ear and having it transmitted to the next person until it ends up with the last person in the room in grotesquely twisted shape. What happened? Not listening well? Lack of adequate vocabulary? Something in communications obviously went awry.

At any rate, communications will always be a problem and

"opening channels," by itself, will not solve it. Adam probably misunderstood Eve, and Eve probably wondered what Adam really meant when he said that he didn't like green apples. But communications can be improved when we learn the art of listening, when communicants establish a true person-to-person relationship, and when all of us acknowledge that we can learn something by listening even to a fool.

6. Bill of Rights for Catholics

Frequent reports of petitions by councils and senates of priests for a study of their theological and canonical position in the church led Professor George Wendel of St. Louis University and me to utilize our "right" of an afternoon coffee-break through several weeks to work on a project we think is important. Following the urging of Vatican II to contribute to the renewal of the church, we set out to formulate a tentative "bill of rights" for Catholics. Our hope is that it will stimulate further thought and discussion to contribute to the renewal and perfection of the church as called for by the council.

Present canon law, which determines the procedural rights and thus the exercise of substantive freedoms of the People of God, was developed in a period when church authority was exercised in military and monarchical fashion. Such law naturally emphasized the power of authority at the expense of the substantive freedoms and procedural rights of individual members of the church — priests, religious, and laity.

While necessary for the time, this formulation of canon law obscured the teaching of Christ and his disciples on the dignity and worth of the human person, and the rights that both protect and flow from the dignity of the human person.

Pope John XXIII called Vatican Council II to adapt the church to a changing society, and the American church is in a unique position to lead the world in following the council's mandate for such adaptation in the area of responsible freedom within the structure of the church. American society has long accepted this principle enunciated by Vatican Council II in its *Declaration on Religious Freedom:*

"It is in accordance with their dignity as persons — that is, beings endowed with reason and free will and therefore privileged to bear personal responsibility — that all men should be at once impelled by nature and also bound by a moral obligation to seek the truth, especially religious truth. They are also bound to adhere to the truth, once it is known, and to order their whole lives in accord with the demands of truth. However, men cannot discharge these obligations in a manner in keeping with their own nature unless they enjoy immunity from external coercion as well as psychological freedom."

We feel that present canon law does not guarantee, and indeed prevents priests, religious, and laity from exercising these freedoms as defined by the Vatican Council.

We therefore suggest as a basis for discussion of freedom within the church the recognition of at least the following fundamental freedoms and rights of all Christians — priests, religious, and laity.

Created to the image and likeness of God, man is a free and responsible being. He therefore is endowed with freedom of conscience, recognized repeatedly by the recent Council, as in the following statement: "On his part, man perceives and acknowledges the imperatives of the divine law through the mediation of conscience. In all his activity a man is bound to follow his conscience faithfully, in order that he may come to God, for whom he was created. It follows that he is not to be forced to act in a manner contrary to his conscience. Nor, on the other hand, is he to be restrained from acting in accordance with his conscience, especially in matters religious."

Another freedom all men possess by reason of their nature is the freedom of inquiry to discover the truth in every discipline, for all truths lead to Truth which will make us free, and men have the consequent freedoms of expression and communication. Vatican Council II summed up this right inherent in man in these words: "Truth, however, is to be sought after in a manner proper to the dignity of the human person and his social nature. The inquiry is to be free, carried on with the aid of teaching or instruction, communication, and dialogue. In the course of these, men explain to one another the truth they have discovered, or think they have discovered, in order to assist one another in the quest for truth."

Freedom of inquiry to discover the truth and freedom to express and communicate it obviously involve the right of priests, religious, and laymen in the church to speak to those in authority and to obtain a sincere hearing. "In the exercise of their rights," Vatican II tells us, "individual men and social groups are bound by the moral law to have respect both for the rights of others and for their own duties toward others and for the common welfare of all. Men are to deal with their fellows in justice and civility."

In adapting to modern society and in recognizing the human dignity of man, the American church could well borrow procedural freedoms from civil common law, which bears a greater imprint of Christian teaching than does canon law. Common law's protections, as applicable to the church, would require that no person shall be deprived of liberty or property, including his right to his good name, without due process of law.

Such due process should include: (1) adequate notice of charges and opportunity to prepare a defense; (2) adequate hearing before an impartial tribunal; (3) the right to counsel; (4) the right to summon witnesses on one's behalf; (5) the right to confront and question accusers and witnesses; (6) the right to a reasonably speedy adjudication of the case; (7) protection against unreasonable punishments; (8) the right of at least one appeal to an impartial tribunal consisting of persons who had no part or interest in the previous proceeding.

Many of the current controversies and problems facing the American church, and indeed the world church, could at least be approached in the spirit called for by Vatican II were there clear recognition of these rights as stated or implied in that Council's documents.

For example, the entire question of the priesthood, including such a subsidiary but important question as the priest's relationship to hierarchical authority, might be approached differently if treated in the light of a more modern context of individual freedoms in a truly post-conciliar church.

There is now urgent need at least for stating safeguards for inquiry into and free discussion of open questions in the church, much as almost every respectable university grants freedom of tenure to professors under certain mutually acceptable conditions. Bishops who refuse such safeguards are simply contradicting what they said collectively at the last ecumenical council of the church.

7. Canon Law Must Fit All Cultures

A revised code of canon law could be the most important accomplishment in the church's renewal. When the new code is formulated, renewal in all areas can be more easily realized or it can be seriously impeded. There are good reasons to hold that church law should not be codified, as Anglo-Saxon common law has never been, but that it should evolve from precedent to precedent.

But the church has used Roman law ever since its early history, a form of law subject to codification, and it is unrealistic to expect that the present Canon Law Commission will not formulate a new code. We can hope, however, that the commission can pay some attention to the impact of Anglo-Saxon law as seen in at least the spirit of Vatican II.

Law grows out of a culture, as the studies of Eichorn on German law and Savigny on Roman law demonstrated more than 150 years ago. This is not accepted as a truism, except by implication, in Rome. The Vatican II Fathers, however, have insisted that the church must transcend all cultures and still be at home in every culture.

The imposition of detailed Roman canon law on the entire church would seem to violate this precept, since it is foreign to all but the Latin culture. This leads to the perplexing problem of how to maintain diversity in unity in the legal expression of ecclesiology. Some leads can be found in the code for the Eastern churches, promulgated piecemeal from 1949 until 1958. It paid some respect to national differences within the Eastern churches, but even here Rome's overriding concern was uniformity.

When Cardinal Pietro Ciriaci, prefect of the Commission for the Reform of Canon Law, died in December, 1966, the Pope named Archbishop Pericle Felici to succeed him. Archbishop Felici seems concerned that conservative curialists want nothing more than slight modifications of the existing code, even though the Commission overrode this plan in favor of a complete re-writing of the code. He speaks of Vatican II as making it possible "to render the new codification more vibrant, more dynamic, more closely bound to the mystery of the church and therefore more conducive to the ultimate goal of the ecclesiastical community, which is the salvation of souls." His comment on the new codification sounded promising when he said that it "will avoid as far as possible a crystallization of the law, which can be said to be innate in every codification which is not continually made more living."

It is not easy to know what such a statement means in Rome. To many Romans it could mean dropping a few obviously archaic canons and inserting a few quotations from Scripture and Vatican II. It is disconcerting that on the Commission there is only one American, a Benedictine who has lived in Rome for twenty years, and there are very few men on it who know anything about Anglo-Saxon law. Even in Rome, the present code of canon law simply does not respect the human person as he is described in the various documents of Vatican II. It is especially galling in the Anglo-Saxon countries where a person is presumed innocent until proven guilty, where he is allowed to know and confront his accusers, where he can summon witnesses, and is entitled to expert legal counsel and other procedural safeguards.

Groping toward a solution of this difficult problem suggests that the Commission for the reform of Canon Law might try to formulate a core code, something like a basic constitution, that could be so generally phrased as to transcend all cultures. It would have to deal with basic human values, with rights and responsibilities based on human nature, but realized differently in different cultures. These are such basic rights as freedom of conscience, access to the means necessary to follow one's vocation, and freedom from discrimination in the culture in which one lives.

The rights and responsibilities of those in authority will also have to be spelled out in quite general terms if they are not to violate the proper autonomy which the Vatican Fathers say each culture should enjoy "within the context of the common good." This could work in some ways like our federal system. The new code could reserve certain powers and authority to Rome, relegating the rest to the national conferences of bishops.

The inherent disadvantage of codification is that it crystallizes the law, to use Archbishop Felici's apt phrase, and soon makes it inapplicable in equity to changing conditions.

Constitutional law, on the other hand, admits of changing interpretations and applications of general principles, thus keeping it relevant to changing social and ecclesiological conditions. In our own American experience, state constitutions which attempted to cover every detail of life became archaic within a few years and have had to be amended often. The national constitution has required relatively few amendments, on the other hand, as its relevance to changing conditions has been maintained by legislation and a body of judicial interpretations.

I am not sure that curial officials understand what the council Fathers meant when they spoke about "the legitimate autonomy of human culture," and said: "Because it flows immediately from man's spiritual and social nature, culture has constant need of a just freedom if it is to develop. It also needs the legitimate possibility of exercising its independence according to its own principles."

It is difficult to see how more than a general constitution for canon law can be written without violating these principles. It seems obvious that each national episcopal conference is the logical body for applying such general principles of a canon law constitution to its own society.

Moreover, such legislation could be more easily amended to meet changing needs than could a detailed set of canons, such as we now have, adopted for the entire Roman Catholic Church. If the reformed canon law is as detailed as the present one, it will survive only if many of the canons are ignored or forgotten as conditions change — which is the case with the 2,414 canons of the present code adopted in 1917.

8. The Challenge to Authority in the Church

Those in positions of authority are on the defensive, and they are not doing a very good job of defending their exercise of authority. There have always been arbitrary wielders of authority in the church, as well as in government, in social groups, and in families. This column is not concerned with them, for they are personality problems outside the pale of rational discussion.

The concern here is rather with those who try to exercise their authority for the good of their subjects and of the church as a whole. Such authority-bearers as bishops, pastors, and religious superiors are genuinely puzzled to find that they are now "bad guys." They cannot understand that their subjects are loyal rather than simply rebellious when they say they cannot obey certain orders, that they must follow their consciences, that authority arbitrarily wielded is neither humane nor Christian.

I suspect that most exercises of arbitrary authority in the church today are the result of insecurity on the part of bishops, pastors, religious superiors, and college administrators. They see looming before them the specter of mass rebellion and ecclesiastical anarchy when a subordinate dares to ask "why," for the old tradition was that "theirs was not to reason why." Such, they thought, is contrary to the Christian virtue of obedience and that exemplary virtue of humility expected of all underlings.

This sense of insecurity which leads to many absurdly arbitrary exercises of authority can best be understood by comparison to the crisis of authority so many fathers experience when their children move from childhood to incipient maturity. When a little child asks "why," the father can well answer "because your father says so." This is the exercise of paternal authority. It is rational; it is fair. As the child advances in age, however, the intelligent father begins to explain the reasons for his decisions. By the time the child has begun to mature he is brought into the decision-making process by the parents — or he rebels.

Generally speaking, ecclesiastical authorities have failed in this respect, and this never really showed up in the past because their subjects acquiesced to living in perpetual childhood. Since Vatican II, and largely because of it, both clerical and lay people have begun to mature religiously and most of those in authority do not know how to handle this new sociological and psychological situation. These subordinates growing out of childhood into maturity are "rebellious" because they no longer think and act like little children.

Thus we have bishops and other religious authorities who hide behind their shield of authority, who make decisions without explanation or consultation because they lack self-confidence and take refuge in the old idea that they are accountable only to their own superiors in the line of command running from God through Rome to the bishops and other religious superiors. This is a concept of authority enshrined by an embattled church at the Council of Trent, which was necessary for the time. This was, in effect, military or absolute paternalistic authority that could brook no discussion, no need for justification, since absolute, unquestioning obedience was requisite. The mentality accepting such authority was that of men interested in the good of the church, but divorced from Christian humanistic norms in favor of those of military law. Such law and such exercise of authority can be justified as a temporary expedient, but not as a permanent state of affairs.

The need for paternalistic and military exercise of authority has passed, as the Fathers at Vatican II recognized. But when they returned to their respective dioceses, many of the Vatican Fathers found it impossible to adopt a new mode of exercising their proper authority. They were like fathers who have to relate to their adult offspring as though they were still little children.

Every society needs persons in authority, as Vatican II recognized, but their way of exercising authority differs according to the age and its culture.

Most of Vatican II's specific remarks on authority were addressed to limitations on secular and political authority. Implicitly, however, were limitations on the exercise of authority by ecclesiastical superiors. The most specific statements were made in the *Decree on the Renewal of Religious Life*. While the Council Fathers were careful to safeguard the authority of religious superiors, as they were of bishops, they counseled that superiors should use their "authority in a spirit of service for the brethren, and manifest thereby the charity with which God loves them . . . Let him [the superior] give the kind of leadership which will encourage religious to bring an active and responsible obedience to the offices they shoulder and the activities they undertake. Therefore a superior should listen willingly to his subjects and encourage them to make a personal contribution to the welfare of the community and of the church."

Those favoring renewal in the church can point optimistically to some bishops and pastors who have created structures for consulting with their subordinates before making decisions. Others have accepted priests' councils that were created spontaneously. But these organizations will be ineffective unless the superiors take a new attitude toward the way they exercise their authority. It will take a generation, I believe, for this to come about.

Meanwhile, we must be tolerant of bishops and other superiors who have the old attitude of authority so ingrained in their nature that they cannot treat their subjects as adults even when they try. We must believe them to be honest when they say they are acting in the interest of their subjects. But we must also point out each abuse of authority, for we must not join the conspiracy of silence that countenanced and implicitly justified arbitrary acts in the past.

9. Pope John Repudiated the Grand Inquisitor

In Dostoevsky's *Brothers Karamazov* the skeptic Ivan tells his religious brother Aloysha about a novel he might write. "The Legend of the Grand Inquisitor" is to be set in Spain in the sixteenth century. Christ comes in human form the day after almost a hundred heretics were burned. He never speaks a word, but everyone recognizes Him. When the Grand Inquisitor sees Christ, he has Him arrested. That night he visits Christ in His cell to explain why He must be executed in the morning.

The Grand Inquisitor berates Christ for having made man free. "I tell Thee that man is tormented by no greater anxiety than to find someone quickly to whom he can hand over that gift of freedom . . . We have corrected Thy work and have founded it upon miracle, mystery, and authority. And men rejoiced that they were again led like sheep, and that the terrible gift that had brought them such suffering, was, at last, lifted from their hearts." Christ had overestimated man in giving him the unsupportable burden of freedom, the Grand Inquisitor maintains, so He must die before He tortures man by freeing him a second time.

The Grand Inquisitor, who strangely earns the reader's sympathy because he bears the torturous burden of freedom alone and sincerely wants to spare his flock, has been repudiated by John XXIII, Vatican II, and Paul VI, and as Catholics face the responsibilities of freedom, many are troubled, insecure, longing for the placid yesterday when decisions were made for them and religion consisted of going through certain motions and prayers formulated by those in authority.

34

Much has been written on the new attitude toward freedom and authority. Much sympathy has been shown to the authority who must make the final decision, such as President Johnson standing alone in his office, or Pope Paul VI kneeling alone in his chapel. The agony of decision-making is great. But I have not seen much written on the similar, though lesser agony of the ordinary priest, nun, or layman who is called upon to make his own free, responsible decision. 1475807

Everybody is in favor of freedom until he realizes that true freedom entails serious responsibilities, and that it does not mean doing whatever he wants to do. Then many (most?) will opt for being told what to do, or think, or say. Many (most?) in positions of authority would like it that way, for it is easier to herd a flock of sheep than tend a group of free men. But we have been given a mandate (to use an "out" word) for freedom, and we have been urged to exercise it responsibly.

In *Pacem in Terris*, Pope John added liberty to truth, justice, and charity as the foundations of society. "Human society," he said, "is realized in freedom, that is to say, in ways and means in keeping with the dignity of its citizens, who accept the responsibility of their actions precisely because they are by nature rational beings." One of the principal functions of authority, he reminded us, is to extend and widen the area of freedom. What he was saying here about political society is obviously true of that society which is called the People of God.

Both authority and freedom are necessary in any society. Without authority there can be no order, and without freedom society cannot be human. There will always be tension between authority and freedom, and the abiding problem will always be where to draw the line between the two. It is easy to say that the ideal is the most extensive freedom compatible with truth, justice, and charity. It is not quite so easy for some to say that this includes the freedom to make mistakes. Nor is it quite so easy for some to admit that the limits of freedom and authority will naturally vary from age to age, and even from person to person.

Perhaps dialogue on freedom and authority would be more fruit-

ful if it centered on the way each was exercised, rather than on
the abstract rights and duties of each. By this time it should
hardly be necessary to remind those in authority that they are
dealing with persons, not with children or with things. Terminol-
ogy of the past, such as "my obedient son" or "the pastor and
his flock," obscures the fact that "son" and "flock" are usually
mature adults who have the inherent right to be treated as such.

Authority would lessen tensions if it were exercised on a face-to-
face level rather than as a dictate from on high. Paradoxically,
those in authority who feel confident and secure are usually much
more humane and much less authoritarian in exercising their
authority.

Tension between authority and freedom would also be lessened
if the responsibility of those acting freely was thoroughly understood. Some who are just a little intoxicated with the call to
freedom forget to follow the example of St. Paul to put off the
ways of a child when they are no longer children. Responsibility
involves the hard work of study, of trying to see things objectively,
before freely making decisions. It involves trying to understand
the position of the person in authority. It involves an absolute
commitment to truth and a true desire to be guided by charity.

The new commitment to accept the burden of freedom given
to us by Christ will cause any number of bumps and bruises in
the days ahead. As they occur, it might be well to remember
the Grand Inquisitor's last words to Christ: "Tomorrow Thou
shalt see that obedient flock who at a sign from me will hasten
to heap up the hot cinders about the pile on which I shall burn
Thee for coming to hinder us."

10. That Ugly Cloud
of Anticlericalism

Several years ago the late Father John Courtney Murray observed that, at most, anticlericalism in this country was a "small cloud on the horizon." Today it looks like a small but ugly cloud over the middle of the country. And it defies the pattern of anticlericalism worked out in other countries and other ages.

Historians used to say that anticlericalism developed only in the wake of clericalism. It was an attitude found among "intellectuals," the middle class, the "liberals," and the more prevalent in Latin than Germanic countries. It was an "ism" for men only. (Women were still docile in these countries, and one of the standard charges of anticlericals was that the priests controlled women through the confessional.) This anticlericalism was directed against the clergy and hierarchy of an established church, against clergy who were authoritarian, suspicious of if not hostile to new ideas and new institutions. The clergy were easily identifiable, and few of them showed any pastoral sense except in rural areas and foreign missions.

Many European anticlericals went to absurd lengths, blaming the clergy — and in time the church, which was identified with the higher clergy — for every ill in society. The clergy responded with similar charges against anticlericals, with the result that clericalism and anticlericalism fed on each other, growing more virulent and vicious throughout the nineteenth century. This anticlericalism made little headway among rural Catholics largely, it seems, because there the clergy were serving people and there they had a sense of community.

37

Anticlericalism failed to develop in this country, as it did in some European countries and in Latin America. The reasons are manifold and complex. Among them, however, the following are prominent. First, the church and the clergy were not identified with the political or social power structure. Second, the clergy rendered real service to the Catholic immigrant. Third, clergy and laity embraced the common task of building churches, schools, hospitals, orphanages, and other institutions. They took common pride and got common satisfaction from what they did together. Fourth, for the most part laymen were so busy earning a living and seeing that their children received more education, more everything than "I had when I was a kid," that they were content to be treated by the clergy in religious life like obedient children. Resentment against priests and bishops did break out in some places, not because they were clergy but because they were the wrong national brand. It was resentment of Irishmen against a German pastor, of Germans against an Irish pastor.

Again, mostly for historical and environmental reasons, relations between clergy and laity were warmest and most cordial in the Midwest. Here there was true person-to-person relationship. Parishes were not large enough to become rigidly institutionalized, and the priests had to rely on laymen for more than financial support.

Then something happened. Some laymen in Oklahoma City openly attack their bishop and engage in character assassination against some of their priests. Catholics in Chicago hatefully jeer at priests and nuns supporting the Negro civil-rights movement. Less publicized but equally vicious attitudes are voiced elsewhere, in living room conversations, in notes dropped into collection boxes, in letters to pastors and editors of Catholic papers.

But this is not the way it was supposed to happen. Those who feared the possibility of anticlericalism in this country thought it would first occur on the east coast, where numbers and older traditions prevented the close person-to-person relationship between clergy and most parishioners. The anticlerical revolt was supposed to occur among "intellectuals" and "liberals." They were proud, they were dangerous. Sometimes they even asked why. But the liberals did not become anticlerical — mostly, I think, because the clergy were catching up with the liberals' thinking.

The anticlerical attitude developed mostly among laymen who refused to accept the social teaching of the church, and it was directed again those bishops, priests, and religious teachers who did. Ironically, this could have been predicted by Karl Marx (whose teaching the clergy are accused of adopting). For the common element in the new anticlericalism seems to be a feeling of insecurity. Lower middle-class home owners in Chicago fear for their investment if the church's racial teaching is implemented in their neighborhood. Upper middle-class Catholics similarly fear for their investments and income if the "liberal" social teaching of the church prevails.

Then came Vatican II. Financial conservatives are usually religious conservatives, and now they have a worthy cause to embrace. Their religious foundations are shaking and they feel terribly insecure. They are sincerely trying to save Holy Mother Church from the clergy who are destroying it. This makes for a selective anticlericalism, which lacks the simplistic consistency of the French, Spanish, or Italian brands. But it has its own inner consistency. It is directed against priests and bishops who become involved in "secular" matters, such as racial justice, and now against the teaching they duped the bishops into promulgating in Vatican II. Whereas the older anticlericalism was directed against the clergy for remaining aloof and identifying with the established power structure, the new American anticlericalism is directed against the priest because he does not remain aloof and identifies instead with "revolution."

Anticlericalism, American style, remains only a small cloud. But the cloud rumbles nosily for its size, and it is an ugly little cloud.

11. NCCC Sought a True Church Cross Section

A valid criticism of the new National Committee on Catholic Concerns is that it does not represent a cross section of the American church. In this meeting of some hundred prominent and concerned Catholics there were hardly any "conservatives" or young people, and only one black person. Thus the "liberals" and "moderates" predominated, and the consensus paper emanating from the NCCC's conference reflected their position rather than that of a true cross section of American Catholics. This is a valid criticism — not of those who met, but of those who did not attend. A true cross section of American Catholics would be predominantly apathetic.

The local arrangements committee in St. Louis, of which I was a member, made every effort to have conservatives, young people, and black Catholics attend this meeting which was called to express Catholic concerns and to form or not to form a federation of Catholic organizations and individuals to do something about them.

Conservatives, generally, showed no interest and, despite repeated invitations, did not attend. So it was with young people and black Catholics. Thus the valid criticism that the group was not truly representative should be leveled against those who did not attend rather than those who did. Apparently those called "liberals" and "moderates" are, with some exceptions, the only Catholics interested in implementing the directives of Vatican II and last year's joint pastoral letter of the American bishops.

When I began a weekly column some years ago I resolved to make it one of reflections on developments in the church and society in which I was not personally involved. Here I breach that resolve because the purpose and the procedure of the NCCC have been so grossly misrepresented and misunderstood that I feel obliged to put its purpose and procedure on record. The overall purpose of the NCCC is to furnish a federation or — if you like — an umbrella under which groups and individuals who have been polarizing into positions to isolate themselves from other Catholics can dialogue and remain open to other attitudes and persuasions.

The NCCC was not organized in opposition to the bishops, nor was it conceived of as any kind of "underground organization." It was thought of as an umbrella organization of Catholics who were active in the institutional church in various organizations in the so-called establishment and whose freedoms were in this way properly limited. In the NCCC, however, they would be independent, concerned Catholics from many disciplines and with many specialized interests who could effect a cross fertilization that would occasionally feed back to the institutional church a consensus of Catholic opinion on various questions. Its purpose, we wrote to the bishops when the consensus paper was sent to them, is to help them "overcome resistance to reform and renewal (in the church)."

The NCCC conference used the American Assembly plan so successfully employed by government and business groups wanting to arrive at a consensus of the group's thinking. A carefully prepared agenda was followed by four groups of about 25 each through four three-hour sessions. A reporter from each group presented the consensus it reached to a chief reporter who collated them into a tentative consensus paper presented to the entire group at the final session. In this three-hour session the statement was edited by 107 "editors," with each proposed modification being adopted or rejected by majority vote. Thus no one endorses every word or phrase or sentence in the final statement (I am unhappy with a number of them), but the final report is an honest consensus of what those who attended the meeting think of the strengths, assets, weaknesses, and problems in the American Catholic Church today.

The group showed itself critical of the bishops in some respects, but what reporters in both the secular and Catholic press apparently missed is that when the consensus criticized the church it was criticizing itself and fellow Catholics, that it was critical of bishops only when it mentioned them specifically.

If I may continue to be personal, one man who came to the conference told me that if this did not work he was going to leave the church, that this was the last resort. The general feeling expressed at the end of the conference was that something greater than anyone expected had happened. Such affirmations may be premature. If reluctant conservatives, militant young people, and concerned black Catholics show themselves willing to dialogue in this group to add their voices to the consensus of American Catholics, then it can achieve its conceived purpose. If they fail to do so then the NCCC will not represent a true consensus of Catholic thinking on church concerns in this country — but the onus of failure will lie on those who did not participate.

A last note. Bishops were invited to drop in and to speak with people at the NCCC conference. One did, a tremendous man whom I need not identify by name, because everyone *au courant* with American ecclesiology knows him by name, and a second one wrote to express his interest. There are still more than 200 bishops who can indicate an interest in a group trying, as they have been advised, to help them "overcome resistance to reform and renewal (in the church)." Thus it remains incumbent on bishops, conservatives, young people, and black Catholics to participate in the renewal of the American church called for by Vatican II and attempted to be implemented by the National Committee on Catholic Concerns. Thus the burden remains on those who criticize rather than participate in what the NCCC is attempting to do.

PART II

The Church Is You

1. How Much Freedom for Students?

For several decades faculties at respectable colleges and universities have been accorded freedom to teach and do research essential to their work. In recent years attention has been given to the freedom of students to learn, and attempts have been made to find what specific freedoms are involved in this freedom to learn in its broadest sense. Developments in psychology and sociology suggest that this is more than freedom to choose courses and teachers, freedom of access to books, to question teachers, and to learn in the narrow academic sense. It is also the freedom, many claim, to whatever experiences are involved in maturing into free, responsible adults.

On specifics of this wider student freedom there is little agreement. Students, naturally, include almost every experience as essential to their freedom. Faculty people tend to sympathize with the student point of view in reverse proportion to the professor's age — though there are notable and vocal exceptions. Administrators, again naturally, take a quite restricted view of student freedom; this is only natural, because they are the persons who have to handle the problems such freedoms create, since some students (like some professors, deans, and parents) will abuse the freedoms they are accorded.

Should students be free to drink in their rooms? Have visitors of the opposite sex? Smoke marijuana, and face the legal consequences, but no university sanctions? Should they have unlimited freedom to attend any classes whenever they choose? Should they be free to organize their own courses and choose their own teachers? If so, should they receive credit for such courses? Should they be free to invite onto the campus any speaker they choose?

It is not difficult to set down vague principles extending academic freedom to more than classroom experience and access to books, and it is a good thing to do so. A joint statement on the government of colleges and universities, issued by the American Council on Education, the Association of Governing Boards of Universities and Colleges, and the American Association of University Professors, contains two paragraphs that seem almost an afterthought in their statement. It lists as the last of four specific rights "the same right to hear speakers of their own choice as is enjoyed by other components of the institution (faculty and administrators)." A few lines earlier this joint statement had warned of difficulties in student participation in university affairs: "The obstacles to such participation are large and should not be minimized: inexperience, untested capacity, a transitory status which means that present action does not carry with it a subsequent responsibility, and the inescapable fact that the other components of the institution are in a position of judgment over the students."

These obstacles differ, it seems to me, in each concrete case of implementing student participation in university affairs. Each case must be judged on its own merits and the problems it involves, because each case involves rights and responsibilities of administrators, faculty, and students. It is easy to say that each should enjoy the greatest freedom compatible with the freedom of the others and the attainment of the purposes of the university. But this is no more revealing than to say that your freedom to swing your arms ends at the tip of my nose.

A 1967 case at St. Louis University illustrates some of the complications in realizing student participation in university affairs. Students in control of the Great Issues Series, open to the public, had run into difficulty the previous academic year for failing to clear their invitation and the time and place of a lecture by the academic French Marxist, Roger Garaudy. An acceptable arrangement was worked out with the administration and endorsed by the local AAUP chapter so that Garaudy could speak in the largest hall on campus. Other activities scheduled for that evening suffered from the lack of know-how and consideration by leaders of the Great Issues Series.

In 1967, therefore, the Series' planners properly tried to clear their selectees and dates with the administration. They were told that Episcopal Bishop Pike and civil rights leader Stokely Carmichael did not qualify to speak in an academic community. As I heard the story, the students accepted the judgment on Bishop Pike but insisted on having Carmichael. Here, I believe, both the administrator in charge and the students were wrong. To deny Bishop Pike the privilege of speaking on a campus because he is not academically qualified is nonsense. He has a Ph.D., a D.D., was invited to join the Center for the Study of Democratic Institutions and attend the Pacem in Terris convention in Geneva.

Having Stokely Carmichael speak is another matter. Administrators have the right not to have their university exploited. Carmichael uses or exploits any occasion he is given to speak. His message is not academic; it is incitation to violence. One can argue that students should be exposed to this sort of thing as part of the learning process. But St. Louis University has a responsibility to the community, and Carmichael could well inflame the neighborhood into violence that would serve no good end. It is an established principle that freedom of expression does not include the right to shout "fire" in a crowded theater. This is close to what Stokely Carmichael does in every talk.

Students have the right to invite onto campus speakers of their choice. A university has the right to protect itself from exploitation and the obligation not to expose its environs to the risk of riot and violence. How does one draw the line in each specific case between these rights and obligations? This is a never-ending problem that will have to be worked out in each institution through experience and the precedents established by such experiences.

Attendance at a university confers upon students the "right to learn," not only in the classroom but also in the corridors, the professors' offices, and in other such ways as listening to invited speakers. But this right to learn is circumscribed in various ways, the line to be drawn in each specific instance by prudence, dialogue, and mutual trust of students, faculty, and administrators. The three components of the University must learn to trust one another so that each deserves the other's trust. Faculty and administrators must let students be free to make occasional mistakes, and students must tolerate an occasional mistake by a professor or an administrator.

2. Student Power and a University's Function

The irresponsible use of "student power" on many campuses is jeopardizing the student's legitimate right to express himself responsibly as a student and a citizen. This irresponsible use of "student power" has provoked equally irresponsible and unintelligent reaction, such as untrained policemen in Madison, Wisconsin, teargassing students simply walking from one classroom to another, and poor old General Hershey proclaiming that student protesters against the draft should be punished by being drafted.

The American Association of University Professors was enough concerned with the problem for its Council to issue a resolution which concluded: "In view of some recent events, the Council deems it important to state its conviction that action by individuals or groups to prevent speakers invited to the campus from speaking, to disrupt the operations of the institutions in the course of demonstrations, or to obstruct and restrain other members of the academic community and campus visitors by physical force is destructive of the pursuit of learning and of a free society."

The Council of the AAUP also approved a joint statement on the rights and freedoms of students which its representatives had drawn up with the National Student Association and three other college associations. This statement asserts that "freedom to teach and freedom to learn are inseparable facets of academic freedom. The freedom to learn depends upon appropriate opportunities and conditions in the classroom, on the campus, and in the larger community."

The joint statement discusses freedom in the classroom, in such student affairs as student publications and student gatherings, and in off-campus activities. The pervading note is that students should have freedom to express themselves vocally, in print, and by such demonstrations as marches and rallies. The sole limit on this freedom is that its exercise must not interfere with the normal prime function of the university, which is the freedom to teach and to learn. Student demonstrations which prevent the normal holding of classes by preventing ingress and egress from rooms or buildings are thus condemned as violating a more important freedom than that of dissent on the campus.

Expression of student dissent can be thus limited and still be effective, as examples at my own university have shown. Some students who felt conscientiously impelled to protest against Air Force recruitment on the campus sat in front of the recruitors' table, but kept open a space for students who wanted to talk to the recruiters. Nor did the protesters attempt to block the doorways or corridors in the building. This is responsible protest which makes its point effectively without interfering with the normal operations of the university.

This last phrase is troublesome. What is included in the "normal operation" of a university, and who is to decide what is "normal"? Is the provision for recruiting by the armed services and by industry a normal function of the university? Personally, I think it is, as long as it is so conducted that it does not interfere with the more basic functions of the university — regular classroom attendance, the operation of the library, and so on. But with whom should the decision on these matters rest? Administrators? The faculty? The students?

Ideally, these policy decisions should be made jointly by representatives of all members of the academic community: the governing board, administrators, faculty, and students. For this reason the joint statement on the rights and freedoms of students states: "As constituents of the academic community, students should be free, individually and collectively, to express their views on issues of institutional policy and on matters of general interest to the student body. The student body should have clearly defined means to participate in the formulation and application of institutional policy affecting academic and student affairs."

This does not mean that students must be voting members of the academic senate, the budget committee, or the committee on rank and tenure. But such academic assemblies and boards should establish clear and open channels of communication with student representatives. Perhaps student representatives should attend the meetings of these bodies, there to voice student opinion on various policies or the lack of them. Their right to vote is not so clear, at least on bodies that deal with long-range academic policy. Most students stay at a university for about four years, and it is questionable whether they should have a vote that could bind the university to a policy or a program for many years after they are gone. On other committees, such as those on student life and discipline, I think, they should have a vote. Conceivably, on some committees they should have a preponderant voice and vote.

At any rate, in any university where the joint statement on student rights and freedoms, subscribed to by the National Student Association, is faithfully adhered to there can be no justification for the irresponsible exercise of "student power" that interferes with the normal functioning of the university, and thus violates the other students' more basic right to learn.

3. *The Intellectual Community Speaks to Itself*

The first national meeting of the Catholic Commission on Intellectual and Cultural Affairs centered its discussion around a paper prepared by the late John Courtney Murray on the Catholic scholar in the modern secular world. That was in 1947, before John XXIII, John Kennedy, and Vatican II. It seemed appropriate to the group to discuss the same topic 21 years later, a "coming-of-age" meeting in St. Louis. This time three papers were discussed, and the meeting was scheduled for two days rather than one.

In the generation between these two meetings a change occurred both in the secular world and in Catholic scholars thinking about it — a change one can sense but not easily describe. Both are more open to each other. The secular world seemed less the enemy to be guarded against and overcome in the last meeting than 21 years ago. There was still tension between the Christian scholar and the secular world in which he lives, but it was not the simple tension of direct opposition. As I remember 21 years ago, there was no consideration of what the secular world might offer the Catholic scholar besides opposition; in this year's meeting it was generally assumed that the Catholic scholar could learn from the secular world as well as find problems in encountering it.

There is reason to question whether the Catholic Commission on Intellectual and Cultural Affairs is as effective as it might be. There is no way of measuring how its discussions enlighten its members and cause them to be more effective and productive scholars and professors. The one notable exception to this question of effectiveness was Monsignor John Tracy Ellis' paper on "American Catholics and the Intellectual Life," delivered in 1955 when Maryville College was host to the CCICA meeting, as it was this year. This paper aroused warm discussion at the meeting, which became heated controversy after appearing in *Thought* and later in book form. It made the Catholic intellectual community take cognizance of its alleged backwardness and tendency toward an anti-intellectual complacency. It was, in Bishop John J. Wright's words, "an unusually important contribution to the interpretation and, perhaps, even the direction of our times on the relationship of Catholicism to American intellectual life." Neither the Catholic intellectual community nor the magisterium has been exactly the same since the publication of Monsignor Ellis' paper.

Does one such paper in a generation justify the existence and mode of operation of a group of intellectuals in the Church? Perhaps. But there is no guarantee that another such paper will be delivered and published in the coming generation. My point is to question whether the CCICA has been too cautious about contacts with the press and the general public, whether, like the bishops, they have not hurt themselves by meeting almost in secret. Such meetings enhance freedom of expression and enable the participants more freely to push back the frontiers of knowledge and opinion than if they were open to the news media which notoriously distort discussions in the interest of circulation.

The position of the Catholic intellectual is clear in some respects. He needs freedom to explore and discuss controversial matters, and this requires a measure of freedom from exposure to the public through the news media. But too much protection from the news coverage puts scholars in the position of meditating powerful ideas which may never enter the current of history. Reform and renewal in the Church and secular society move at such a pace that CCICA is called upon to reconsider its methods of relating to the larger Catholic community and our

American society. Scholars in the CCICA, in my opinion, should show a greater courage in entering their contributions into the mainstream of Catholic thought and not worry about the anathemas — which are not as likely to come as they were 21 years ago. These are men who are sufficiently accredited that they can, like Monsignor Ellis over a decade ago, survive criticism, bruised but unscathed.

As an individual who was chairman of the CCICA when Monsignor Ellis made his significant contribution to the Catholic dialogue in 1955, I would like to suggest that this organization is too selective in admitting members and making contact with the mainstream of Catholic thought to be as effective as its potential indicates it could be.

4. Why Enfranchise the 18-Year-Olds?

Young people between 18 and 21 have suddenly become popular with politicians. The Missouri legislature is considering a measure to extend the vote to this age group, and both majority leader Mansfield and minority leader Dirksen have endorsed a federal constitutional amendment to the same effect.

One need not be cynical to decide that 18-to-21-year-old people have become the politicians' loving concern simply because there are and will be so many of them, enough to swing many an election if they were solidly in one political camp or another. Anyone who knows people in this age group could tell the politicians how naïve they are to think that its several million members will vote en bloc for the party that "gives them the vote." But this is beside the point. The question is whether 18 is a truer age than 21 for marking the maturity that should entitle a citizen to vote responsibly.

Until 1944 all 48 states set 21 as the minimum age for voting. Conscription of 18-year-olds during World War II produced the sentiment that anyone old enough to fight and die for his country was old enough to have a voice in setting its policies by voting. In 1943, 31 state legislatures considered proposals to lower the minimum age for voting, and in the following year Georgia reduced the age to 18. Ten years later Kentucky set the same minimum age. The Alaskan constitution set the age at 19, and Hawaii adopted 20 as the minimum age for voting. The remaining 46 states still have 21, but some of them consider lowering the age to 18.

The arguments advanced for lowering the age are usually specious, though appealing, and are far from the best arguments that could be used. The standard sentimental argument is that if young people 18 can be drafted, they should not be denied the vote. This is nonsense. It would follow that only males passing a physical examination are qualified to vote. Young men 18 to 21 make the best trainees for modern warfare. They are strong, malleable, and easier than older persons to indoctrinate. They are more readily inclined to violence, and most of them are heroically courageous. In short, they make the best kind of soldiers. But these are hardly qualifications for voting maturely and responsibly. If anything, they are more likely to be disqualifications unless they are countered and balanced by other traits that many people in all age groups lack — rationality, restraint, objectivity, concern with the welfare of others.

In the abstract, a person is qualified to vote when he is mature enough to vote responsibly on the basis of knowing the issues involved and the candidates' qualifications. Many people never reach this maturity. Others reach it at widely differing ages. Since it is impracticable as well as undesirable to set up individual tests — like former literacy tests in several Southern states — some arbitrary figure, such as the minimum voting age, must be set. It should be the age at which most people become qualified to vote maturely and responsibly.

Is 18 a better age than 21? A number of considerations can be advanced in favor of it, much more compelling arguments than the facetious one advanced by politicians. One consideration is that most young Americans today are better informed about their government and its problems than were their predecessors, even at 21. More attention is given in school to American institutions, to domestic issues and problems of foreign policy than in the past. In other words, most young men and women are better equipped now to vote at 18 than in the past.

A second consideration in favor of voting at 18 is that young people are more interested and more concerned with political and social affairs than ever in the past. Until about 1960 most young people were interested only in making money or following an individual vocation. Since then, however, and especially since President Kennedy engaged them, they have shown a lively interest in social concerns. Such involvement qualifies them, at least in some measure, to have a vote on public policy and the candidates who will formulate it.

But there is a compelling counter-argument: that most young people in this 18 to 21 age bracket are not yet psychologically and intellectually mature enough to cast a responsible vote. This was the age group that vociferously and violently supported Hitler and Mussolini. This was the group, together with those through 24, that Chancellor Schuschnigg wanted to exclude from the plebiscite on whether Austria should become part of Nazi Germany. This is the age group rampaging through China today as the Red Guards.

These are the youth of other times and other lands. Can the same addiction to impulsive and violent behavior be postulated of the American youth today? We find them in large numbers in urban riots, peace and war demonstrations, civil rights and anti-civil rights outbursts, in Vietnam "teach-ins" and picket lines against such teach-ins. Perhaps they are so noticeably present because they have so much physical vitality and time on hand not possessed by older people. They add up to a rather small fraction of the age group, I suspect, and probably are not representative of the group as a whole, But they cannot be overlooked when we discuss the qualifications of this age group for voting maturely and responsibly.

My present position is that it would be a mistake to pass another constitutional amendment denying states the right to exclude those 18 or more from voting, as states may not deny the vote because of race, religion, or sex. Constitutional amendments should not be on relatively minor issues; when they are mistakes they are not easy to repeal, as our forebears discovered with the prohibition amendment. It is much more reasonable to have states take the initiative in lowering the age qualification for voting.

One advantage of the federal system is that individual states can experiment with different arrangements, which other states and even the national government can adopt if they prove good. If they do not, they can be abandoned without great trauma. Instead of a constitutional amendment, then, it seems wiser for states to follow the lead of Georgia and Kentucky, and for political scientists to watch the results closely so as to recommend similar action by the rest of the states, or dissuade them from it. My guess is that enfranchising 18- to 21-year-olds will have about as much effect on the electorate as the enfranchisement of women by the nineteenth amendment — hardly any.

5. *League of Women Voters*

It can be argued quite well that "voter education and sophistication is the only cure" of freeing foreign policy from domestic politics. Now let us see one organization which tries to apply this cure: The League of Women Voters. Women getting the vote does not seem to have made much difference, but the story of how they got the vote is interesting — filled with righteous indignation, pathos, comedy, and occasionally just plain nonsense.

The case for women voting was presented first in Anglo-Germanic countries, such as England, the United States, Germany, and the Scandanavian countries, and only very recently in the Latin countries where woman's role was confined to the home as wife, mother, cook, and hostess. When the franchise was widened to include all adult males, and when women achieved greater literacy and entered the business world, it was only natural that the question of extending the franchise to women was raised.

Arguments for and against their getting the franchise were as a rule equally silly. The German Communist August Bebel, for example, campaigned for women suffrage because he believed that all women would vote the Communist ticket when they learned that in bourgeois society they were unpaid kitchen and bedroom slaves. In Spain conservatives, who ordinarily opposed female suffrage, and liberals, who ordinarily supported it, changed positions in the 1930's because both believed the women's confessors would tell them how to vote — and most priests were conservative. In England, John Stuart Mill argued for female suffrage because he believed women were rational (good for a roar in the House of Commons), and because he married a strong-

minded widow with whom he had long been in love and who
insisted on women's right to vote. Most Englishmen and Americans who argued for female suffrage, however, took the rather
romantic stand that this was the only way to clean up politics
and achieve thwarted reform (something like scrubbing the
kitchen).

Arguments against women voting were similarly unrealistic.
The most general were two: (1) politics is dirty business (saloons
and smoke-filled rooms) and women should not soil themselves
by getting into it; (2) women are good at needlework and other
such things, but they just don't and can't understand political
issues. But women were not to be denied — at least in the non-
Latin countries where they could not understand how Madame
Pompadour did not have to cast a ballot to influence French
politics, as Latin women well understood. So women in England
and America undertook campaigns to get the vote: lying in
front of streetcars and omnibuses, forcing husbands to address
political gatherings in their favor, using hatchets, and making
general nuisances of themselves. So they got the right to vote.

The decisive event in both countries was their participation
in World War I, which doesn't really prove a thing about
their qualification for the franchise. Somehow it was reasoned
that women's committed work as nurses and relief workers in
the war entitled them to vote. In 1918 the English government
gave women over 30 the vote (one suspects in the hope that
few women would admit to such a devastating condition), and
10 years later it was extended to all women on the same basis
as men. In the United States, of course, the right to vote is
a matter controlled by each state. Wyoming and other western
states were the first to enfranchise women, who were cherished
rarities in these areas, and finally in 1920 the federal constitution
was amended to forbid any state to deny the vote because of sex.

So women got the right to vote. What difference did it make?
Not very much. A few men wryly observed that women probably
voted heavily for handsome Warren Harding in 1920, the first
election after the ratification of the nineteenth amendment. Some

other disgruntled men blamed women in states where they could vote before 1920 of pushing the prohibition amendment. But women seem generally to have voted about like men.

The best thing to come out of the suffrage movement is the League of Women Voters, conceived in the Statler Hotel in St. Louis in 1919 and organized on a national basis a year later in Chicago. It was conceived at the convention of the American Woman's Suffrage Association when President Carrie Chapman Catt departed from her prepared keynote address to call upon members to "raise up a league of women voters." While the convention was still in session word was ecstatically received from Jefferson City that Missouri had ratified the nineteenth amendment.

The convention decided to organize such a league as Mrs. Catt had called for and, after considering different titles, agreed to call it "The League of Women Voters." Because of the solidarity they had forged as the American Woman's Suffrage Association they apparently felt that women would turn out *en masse* to vote and would somehow all vote for reform, for the right candidates, for good government. Of course it did not happen that way, as ladies of the League found in the presidential election of 1920.

The League of Women Voters survived this and subsequent disappointments, however, to become perhaps the best organization in American political life. Their activity soon convinced skeptics that a nonpartisan organization was possible, and that it could endorse issues without endorsing candidates. The League has scrupulously followed a three-pronged program of (1) voter education, (2) getting out the vote, and (3) taking a stand on issues.

Voter education is perhaps the most important of these programs. The League does considerable research, invites all candidates to address its members, and publishes reports on issues its committees have studied. Getting out the vote, of course, is a frustrating task, and there is no way of knowing how many women who would not have otherwise voted are shepherded into polling places by the League. As for taking a stand on issues, such as nonpartisan election of judges and support of the United Nations, the League of Women Voters has a record second to none for sanity, balance, objectivity, and good judgment.

Does the League have weaknesses? Perhaps it does not have enough members who are "persuaders." In over 45 years it has not been able to sell itself widely to the rest of American women. Maybe this is the fault of American women generally rather than that of the League of Women Voters. Men might do well to follow its studies and recommendations. After all, since we let them vote, why not profit from it?

6. Washington Bogeyman Still a Phantom

Discussion of New Deal measures 30 years ago down to arguments about medicare yesterday and federal aid to education today always conjures up the phantom bogeyman of a national government that wants to do everything and control every aspect of our lives. It is difficult to explain the mind that conjures up this bogeyman except on the grounds of political ignorance.

Employees in the national government increased from 2,020,-000 in 1950 to 2,213,000 in 1960, whereas employees in state and local governments increased from 4,285,000 to 6,387,000 for the same period. The latest available figures list 2,528,000 employees of the national government, and 7,536,000 in state and local government.

Federal expenditures increased from $39.5 billion in 1950 to $76.5 billion in 1960, about 40 percent of this for national defense. In the same period state and local government expenditures increased from $22.8 billion to $51.9 billion. Thus we see that state and local governments have been growing much more rapidly than the national government in expenditures, in employees and apparently, therefore, in functions and services.

True, the national government does many things that it never did in the past, and that most of us wish it did not have to do. There are two principal reasons why it has assumed numerous new functions. The first is that the growing complexity of American society and the economy have made local or state regulatory functions obsolete and ineffective. Flood control, irrigation, and power projects, for example, usually cross state boundaries and must become federal projects — or else not be done at all. The TVA is an outstanding example of a project that could be handled by no level of government except the federal.

The second reason why the federal government has had to assume certain functions which ideally we would prefer to see handled on the state and local level, is that the lower echelons of government simply defaulted. Many states neglected their highways and ignored the need for urban renewal, adequate support for orphans, widows, the disabled, the unemployed. Private groups, such as relatives, doctors and hospitals, failed to provide adequate care for the aged and other indigent groups. This created a vacuum into which the federal government had to enter.

Those who fear the bogeyman in Washington frequently invoke the principle of subsidiarity which was expressed by Lincoln and spelled out by Pope Pius XI: "Just as it is wrong to take from the individual and hand over to the community what the individual can accomplish by his own initiative and enterprise, in the same way it is an injustice, a grave evil, and a disturbance of right order to transfer to a greater and higher society what can be effected by smaller and lower groups." The principle is sound, practically a truism, but it is difficult to find the federal government violating it when it performs necessary functions not being efficiently or adequately taken care of by the family, the local community, or local and state governments.

As a matter of fact, the federal government seems much more conscious of this principle than governments on the lower levels and private institutions. Most of its social security programs are administered by the states; not by their demand, but by the insistence of the federal government. Washington has provided that local groups administer federal funds in the war on poverty. The federal government was reluctant to administer civil rights laws, and did so only when some of the states patently refused to do so. It set up a commission on intergovernmental relations which tries to allocate various functions to state and local governments, but it has had practically no success in getting these lower levels of government to accept any functions offered to them.

Thus we are faced with the curious situation of those who cry loudest about centralization making it more and more necessary, and meanwhile imputing to Washington the desire to become a Leviathan.

Most federal projects are carried out by state and local governments, but the federal government sets certain standards which must be met to receive federal funds. This is the sensitive spot for those who fear federal domination. I submit that if such minimal standards were not set, Washington would be guilty of the sloppy spending of my taxes. I cannot find any tyranny in setting standards for highway construction or public housing. The federal government has consistently been less inclined to dictate terms for its grants to universities and colleges than have some of the private foundations.

It must be admitted that there are obtuse bureaucrats in Washington, as there are elsewhere, and that some of them want to be empire builders. But this is the human situation. Very few institutions have been willing to lie down and die when their purpose was accomplished. The March of Dimes, for example, did not dissolve when polio was finally conquered. This charge of self-perpetuation and empire-building is really a charge against human nature rather than the federal government.

There is a danger that the phantom bogeyman in Washington can become a real bogeyman. The revolution in cybernetics has made this possible. Within a short time the federal government can easily have a complete dossier on everyone in the country. This is a possibility against which we should be eternally vigilant. But right now it is the federal government which protects us from the neglect of state and local governments, and from the tyranny of some of them — little but real bogeymen.

As yet the bogeyman in Washington remains a phantom. The more vigorous and responsible state and local governments become, the less likely it will be that the phantom will materialize into reality. Orwell's *1984* is now closer to materializing in a southern town or a rural county than in Washington.

7. Decency is the Only Guard for Privacy

Senator Edward Long's Senate Judiciary Subcommittee on Administration Practice and Procedure has revealed the extent to which the citizen's right to privacy is being violated. Some federal agencies have consistently violated the two sections of the 1934 Federal Communications Act which restrict wiretapping and eavesdropping. They have "bugged" offices, hotel rooms, and homes. Business people have planted listening devices in competitor's offices, and private detectives have used such devices to gather information for divorce proceedings, one of them even being a double agent employed independently by a husband and wife to "bug" the other spouse.

Many questionnaires given to job applicants both in government and in business include questions that disturb the inmost areas of privacy and have no proven relevance to the applicant's fitness for the job or his reliability. Perhaps the most flagrant violators to one's right to privacy are the news media, with reporters and television cameras being indecently callous in pushing themselves on grief-stricken women and children when the father of a family has been killed.

A defense — but not a very good one — can be made for every kind of violation of privacy. Newsmen argue that the public has a right to information; government agencies argue that they must be sure of the reliability of employees, and that there is no other way to obtain evidence against criminal syndicates; business people argue that the other firm does it too. But does the public's right to information include the right to know whether a slain policeman's young son also wants to be a policeman? Does the right to test a job applicant's fitness include questions about a 17-year-old typist's sex experiences and how much she enjoyed them?

It is difficult to know where and how to draw the line between one's right to privacy and the right to information on the part of the public, the government, one's spouse, and one's employer. One generally accepted principle is that persons who enter certain careers or positions automatically surrender a measure of their right to privacy. We have a greater right, for example, to know about the President's health than about yours. And somehow it has been established by custom that actors and other public figures have surrendered a good deal of their privacy to their public. But I cannot see where this includes the right to know how long the President's incision was or precisely what Joe Dimaggio's feelings were when he heard of Marilyn Monroe's death.

Ultimately, the right to privacy rests on the rather shaky foundation of American sense of decency, and of outrage when this right is violated. It is not expressly guaranteed in the Constitutional Bill of Rights. The closest article to express anything like the right to privacy is the first half of the sentence that is Amendment IV: "The right of the people to be secured in their persons, homes, papers, and effects, against unreasonable searches and seizures, shall not be violated . . . , " but the second half of that sentence indicates that the framers of the amendment had John Doe warrants in mind.

The Supreme Court consistently treated the Fourth Amendment in this sense. By a 5–4 decision, for example, the court held in 1928 that the Fourth Amendment did not prohibit wiretapping, because this did not involve physical intrusion into the defendant's premises. But the more recent decision invalidating Connecticut's birth control law forbidding married people to use contraceptive devices rested on the principle that this was an undue violation of their right to privacy. Legal opinion is divided on whether this same principle, which rests on a wider view of the right to privacy than physical intrusion into the premises, can be applied to wiretapping, hidden cameras, and other such devices. And it would stretch the Fourth Amendment far beyond its original intent if it were applied to public places, to employment questionnaires, polygraphs, and countless other violations of privacy.

Legislation against violations of privacy is most difficult to write, and the most it can do is make such violations more difficult to perpetrate. No single law can cover wiretapping, bugging, secret cameras, questionnaires, polygraphs, and other devices that violate privacy. Moreover, technological advances are so revolutionary that specific laws limiting or forbidding certain devices would be outmoded within a few years. How can laws be written so that the area of privacy is not the same for all? Finally, how can legislation be drawn up to permit government agencies to use listening devices and polygraphs where national security is at stake, but not use them offensively and scurrilously, as delving into the sex life of a typist in a nonsensitive agency, or bugging lavatories?

If attainable, of course, legal prohibitions against the violation of privacy are the best approach because they carry sanctions for their enforcement. In lieu of legislation, the most effective check on violations of privacy would be an expressed sense of outrage by the American public. Even if no legislation can be formulated by Senator Long's subcommittee, the publicity of his hearings have made us aware of the violations of privacy. Even if the theological concept of human dignity and its accompanying right of privacy cannot be spelled out in legal terms, most Americans have this concept and hold it dear. What they need to do is express their outrage at its violation, whether by the government, by business firms, or by the highly competitive news media.

8. Problems of Cities, Integration Are the Same

Integration is generally considered the nation's most serious domestic problem. Recently, mayors of many big cities told congressmen that saving the inner cities of large metropolitan areas is our most serious problem. These two statements are not contradictory. They say practically the same thing in different words.

For the center of the Negro integration problem now lies in the big cities, where more than half the nation's Negro population lives. Cities cannot be renewed and stabilized unless integration is accomplished, and integration of urban Negroes cannot be accomplished unless the inner cities are renewed and stabilized.

This will take billions of dollars, and most of it will have to be furnished by Washington. But money is only the *sine qua non* of the integration problem, which is far more complex than a simple funding problem.

Prejudice is part of the problem, of course, but not as great a part as we used to think. The really prejudiced people in the cities turn out to be a small fraction as compared with those who fear integration because it might disturb their security.

If the integration movement could be so handled that whites did not fear for their jobs and their homes, what is a derivative prejudice would practically disappear. Even worse than prejudice is apathy — apathy on the part of the vast majority of white people, and apathy (for different reasons) of a majority of the Negro population. And no one has discovered the secret of arousing apathetic masses to a cause with which they should be concerned.

For those who are interested, the problem of integration be-comes a complex of interrelated problems that ultimately reduce themselves to making it possible and desirable for each Negro person to enter the mainstream of American society. Each entry will be something like baptism: a personal decision on the part of the Negro to enter this society, and a welcome reception of him as an equal by those already in it, both white people and their black brethren.

Meanwhile, there seem to be four principal intermediate prob-lems, or perhaps approaches to the ultimate solution of the integra-tion problem. They are: (1) open housing, (2) quality educa-tion, (3) equal job opportunity, and (4) stabilizing Negro family life in the inner city. None of these problems can be solved until they are all solved.

How can an unemployed Negro exercise his right to purchase or rent a decent home in the suburbs? How can an illiterate or undereducated Negro qualify for a good job? How can children in an impoverished, fatherless family stay in school to qualify for a good job to be able to live in a decent home and raise a stable family? There are, of course, heroic individuals who overcame all these obstacles to become respectable Negro edu-cators, lawyers, doctors, and engineers. But for each such heroic individual who worked his way out of the Negro ghetto how many more are born in it and destined to end their existence in it?

Open housing is most difficult to achieve, except in small neighborhood areas where stable integration can and has been accomplished by well educated and relatively prosperous whites and blacks. City open-housing laws still tend to drive white people into the all-white suburbs. State open-housing laws fail where they are most needed, in the metropolitan community that sprawls across state lines. Any national open-housing law will be so watered down that it will accomplish little, and Congress may well pull the old trick of not funding its enforcement adequately.

No one can very well deny that high quality education should be made available to every qualified Negro child. This requires some doing with the neighborhood public school system, and certainly it cannot be done by the inner city itself until other problems, such as good job opportunities and stabilized family life are on their way to being solved.

Headway can be made immediately in improving the Negro's right to equal job opportunity. Federal funds can be withheld from any agency or enterprise that fails in this respect. And preference in job training can be given to the poorest, who in the inner cities are mostly Negroes.

The widely publicized Moynihan report said that "the deterioration of the Negro family . . . is the fundamental source of the weakness of the Negro community at the present time." I prefer "a fundamental source" to "the fundamental source," but that is beside the point. More than one Negro family in four in the cities is fatherless; nearly a fourth of Negro births are illegitimate.

The pattern of breakdown is always the same. The father cannot find a decent job. His wife can usually find some kind of work. The male loses his self-respect, as well as the respect of his children. At this point he deserts his family, frequently to make it eligible for Aid to Dependent Children. Children of these broken families become school dropouts and job dropouts, thus closing off any opportunity to climb the social and economic ladder. There is no reason why programs cannot be devised to help keep the Negro husband at home instead of driving him away from it.

These programs of better job opportunity, open housing, better education, and stabilized family life must all be pursued simultaneously. But there is the danger of their becoming institutionalized, depersonalized, bureaucraticized, helping the Negro as a helpless child.

Ultimately, integration means person-to-person relationship between people of both colors. Why could some white families not adopt a Negro family, try to help them see to their children's education, help them learn about credit and such matters,

help them stay out of trouble? Why not help them see how
they can avoid being exploited? Both white and black families
will suffer disappointments, but there could be many cases of
true integration. Maybe a successful black family could help a
less fortunate white family.

9. Reflections on Riots

Reflection on rioting and lawlessness has led politicians, sociologists, and other concerned persons to study what measures are needed to prevent riots and control them. No politician or journalist seems to have taken seriously the remark of the militant H. Rap Brown that violence is "as American as cherry pie." There is reason to believe that this is becoming true — among whites as well as Negroes. Rough and ready violence are extolled in advertising ("be a healthy animal," etc.), in athletics, entertainment and business, even in the social amenities and the erosion of good manners: some now slap hands, for example, instead of shaking.

This underlying erosion of the amenities and manners that have kept our society relatively orderly needs serious attention. It is creating an environment conducive to spontaneous rioting, looting, maiming, and killing. President Johnson's Commission on Civil Disorders needs on its staff some sociologists, psychologists, and psychiatrists to probe this underlying stratum of violence as well as such obvious measures as open housing and full employment. Sophisticated studies on crowd behavior are currently throwing much light on mob violence in history, and they can suggest methods of preventing mob violence in the future.

Other more specific observations seem in order. The point has been made that the riots are not really racial. Negroes looted Negro stores and killed other Negroes, it is true, and white people were among the rioters and looters. But such an observation overlooks the fact that the riots were partly racial in that the frustrated persons ready to riot were mostly Negroes who suffered more than whites from poor housing, undereducation, unemployment, and broken families. It is too slick to dismiss them as not being racial, just as it is too slick to see them simply as another manifestation of racism.

A second observation is that most of the participants were younger single persons. Employed heads of families did not participate, and insofar as they could they deplored the violence of their neighbors. This is an indictment of Negro and white leaders who refused to take the Moynihan report seriously, for this study found broken homes the basic cause of failure of Negroes to progress in education and employment.

A third observation is on the petty use of the riot crisis by politicians seeking to discredit opponents and to advance their own cause. Senator Dirksen was either hypocritical or stupid — or likely both — in blaming the Johnson administration for the riots. The Senator did as much as anyone to promote them when he fought valiantly to pare down or kill President Kennedy's and President Johnson's bills for urban renewal and similar measures. Congressmen who laughed to death a rat control appropriation bill, who voted noisily for space exploration appropriations and denied small fractions of the same amount to urban affairs, must share the blame for what has happened in many cities. Their answer is enthusiastic support of strong measures to put down riots they have fomented. This is, unfortunately, a reflection on the mood of their constituents — which means most of us socially and morally unenlightened Americans.

Unfortunately, President Johnson was originally almost as petty as Senator Dirksen in repeatedly downgrading a potential rival, Governor Romney, as incapable of handling the situation in Detroit. While President Johnson took time to drive home his political point, houses burned and men were killed. Romney had to fight for his political reputation by claiming that the hesitation and shilly-shallying of which Johnson accused him occurred in Washington after he had asked for federal troops. Such bickering among politicians while stores and homes burned and innocent bystanders were killed reveals an inherent weakness in the American democratic system, for the politicians tried to turn a tragedy into a political asset. There is just no time for a public opinion survey while snipers are killing firemen and children, but apparently elective officials cannot act decisively until public opinion has been polled.

Still another reflection must be made on the role played by the communications media in making riots epidemic. This is an imponderable and truly insoluble problem. Television, radio, and the press are highly competitive industries, and they are essential for an informed citizenry in a democratic country. The common good, however, requires that they accept certain restrictions in the interest of peace and order. What these restrictions are no one can easily say. My opinion is that the coverage of these terrible events tends to make riots and violence epidemic, at least more so than they would have been otherwise. TV pictures made it exciting, almost like barkers at a carnival telling potential customers the thrills of each attraction. The combined coverage of television, radio (the young carry transistors), and newspapers gave the impression that you have to riot if you're with it. TV pictures of looters having a field day and newspaper stories of the loot market certainly must have encouraged young people in other cities to get things going.

Under all these riots, however, the most important cause is the environment of violence we have been developing in recent years. It is accepted more and more as the normal way of life, as good clean fun, "as American as cherry pie." And who can be against cherry pie?

10. Medicare is Qualified Success

In the first year of its existence Medicare proved to be neither the monster described by the AMA nor the benevolent genie conjured up by some of its advocates. Dire predictions that doctors and hospitals would lose their professional independence were not realized, nor were the hospitals inundated with a flood of elderly persons predicted by many doctors — who alone could create that flood.

About 7 of the 19 million persons over 65 took advantage of one or another of Medicare's provisions at a total cost somewhat over $3 billion. This amount exceeded the original estimates, largely because of the sharp increase in hospital charges and doctor fees. Hospital charges rose 16.5 percent, and doctors' fees 7.8 as contrasted with the previous annual average of 3 percent. Other factors than Medicare payments account for part of this sharp increase: higher wages for nurses and hospital employees, and increased cost of equipment and medicines. Many doctors previously charged indigent elderly people less than normal fees, which they properly increased under Medicare. Nevertheless, there was price gouging by some doctors even as they complained bitterly about Medicare.

After a year most hospitals welcome Medicare and most doctors tolerate it, although the new president of the AMA insisted his organization "does not support or indorse it." The biggest complaints have been about the amount of time wasted on paperwork and the length of time before receiving payment. Both were consistently reduced through the year, and Medicare officials promise that they will be even further cut down as this big operation continues to be simplified. Doctors who insist on billing patients directly complicate matters because many elderly people fill out the Medicare forms incorrectly. Many of them have to borrow money to pay the doctor first in order to obtain a receipt to send to Medicare in order to be reimbursed for the doctor's fee.

Despite these shortcomings, which have been somewhat mitigated, Medicare can be judged a qualified success after its first year of operation. One cannot measure precisely what its effects have been on the health of elderly persons, but many have received treatment and had operations they could not have otherwise afforded. Many more have been treated with the dignity of private patients and by doctors of their own choice, whereas they would otherwise have been indigent clinic patients used primarily in the education of interns and residents. Medicare requirements are reported to have raised the standards of medical care of all patients in the nearly 97 percent of hospitals in the nation using it.

Medicare has also had some beneficial indirect results. It has given strong impetus to racial integration. It has also relieved most people over 65 from the nagging worry of the financial burden of serious illness. It was devised to insure the elderly against the disaster of serious illness, not to assume the total cost of their medical care, and it seems to have achieved its purpose.

There are still some problems and issues to be resolved. Paperwork must be further reduced. The time between billing Medicare and receiving payments must also be reduced so that hospitals can operate on a sounder financial basis and patients will not be forced to go into debt to pay their medical bills. The medical profession will have to find replacements for the former elderly clinic patients who can now receive private or semi-private care, because the examination and treatment of human beings must be included in a doctor's education. Again, hospitals maintain that they will have to raise their other charges if Medicare continues to pay only for the costs directly related to the care of beneficiaries. Hospitals average out the per diem costs of all patients so as to cover intensive care and other expensive operations, but Medicare officials claim their patients should not have to pay for maternity and other services they do not receive. (This is a curious reversal of position by both parties on the sharing of costs.)

Medicare is here to stay. Whether it should be extended is the question. The AMA and most doctors fight any attempt to extend its coverage as furthering socialized medicine. They stand on the principle that health care is a privilege rather than a right, that the recipient is responsible for his own medical care, and that no party should intervene in the personal and financial doctor-patient relationship. They consider medical care a service they sell to patients at a price acceptable to both parties. Most doctors are also willing to serve the unfortunate and poor, but on conditions of their own choosing.

Officials in the Health, Education, and Welfare Department want to extend medical care to disabled persons under 65, and in time to widows, children, mothers, and others financially unable to pay for medical services. They stand on the principle that medical care is a human right which the government must furnish if the individual cannot do it himself.

Either principle — that medical care is a privilege or that it is a right — can be carried too far. The operation of Medicare this past year indicates that we can choose some or none of many programs in the spectrum between laissez-faire medical practice and completely socialized medicine. Each program should be discussed and adopted or rejected on its own merits, not on abstractions picturing malicious monsters or benevolent, all-powerful genii. No extension of Medicare will be either of these.

The Church in the Modern World

PART III

The Church in the Modern World

1. Was Pope Pius XII
a Progressive?

History writing about events and people swings like a pendulum.
A Roosevelt or a Kennedy is usually adulated immediately after
his death. Then a harsh reaction sets in, and this is followed by
a more objective assessment lying somewhere between the two
extremes. Pope Pius XII is now being harshly judged as the
severe aristocrat, the man who told Jesuits not to smoke, the
Pope who was unconcerned about people who were not Catholics. Such a view loses sight of the fact that Pius XII was a
progressive innovator, and that his pontificate will eventually be
judged the one in which the decisive turn toward reform and
renewal took place.

Pius XII saw the need of continual adaptation by the church
to be relevant to a changing world. "Certainly the church is a
living organism," he wrote, "and, therefore, in those things which
pertain to the sacred liturgy it grows and develops and conforms
itself to the circumstances and requirements of various times."
He similarly observed that "religious organizations best serve the
needs of the times when, on occasion, without giving up their
own peculiar spirit, they adapt themselves to changing conditions."

Less than two months after the outbreak of World War II,
Pius published his first encyclical, *Summi Pontificatus*. In it he
touched on many points which read like statements of Vatican II
or Paul VI. He expresses gratitude to men of goodwill outside the visible church, stresses the unity of mankind and
wrongness of selfish nationalism. He tells us that complete victory in war bears with it the savage temptation of an imposed
peace, which will be no peace at all.

In this same encyclical he pledges the church's respect for all cultures, tells us that the state will have to undertake more functions than in the past, and that society is designed by the Creator for the "harmonious development and the natural perfection of man."

These ideas of adaptation were put into practice as he reconstructed the church after the war. Strangely, conservatives who resist change in the church now look back on Pius XII's pontificate with nostalgia. Conservatives, as I remember them in those years, were complaining about how Pius XII was taken in by Communists, for he was so radical as to endorse warmly the United Nations and UNESCO. Only a stupid Catholic or unpatriotic American, they held, could accept the UN, and collaboration with UNESCO was a declaration of war against God, religion, and morality. Nevertheless, the Pope had a representative at UNESCO headquarters and made an annual contribution to its expenses. Pius XII even went so far as to say that the UN was a step in the right direction and that it should be strengthened. He also suggested that the countries of Europe should federate.

In his Christmas message of 1944, devoted to democracy, Pius XII distinguished between Rousseauvian democracy which makes the majority absolute, and a sound democracy which recognizes and respects the citizen's inalienable rights. He suggested that if the people had been allowed to participate effectively in the governments of the European totalitarian countries "the world would not have been dragged into the vortex of a disastrous war, and that to avoid the repetition of such a catastrophe in the future we must vest efficient guarantees in the people themselves."

The Pope also took a progressive, positive stand on social and economic life. To mention but two topics, he discussed the role of women in the modern world and the problem of automation in words that sound post- rather than pre-Vatican II.

He urged women's religious communities to modernize their habits and streamline their organizations. He accepted the many groups of laywomen that were springing up after the war to meet specific needs, and he exempted them from canon law requirements for religious bodies. In an address on "Women's Duties in Social and Political Life" Pius explained that in the modern world many women will not be married, nor do they have a vocation to the religious life. For them there is a third vocation to social, professional, or other work whereby they can perfect themselves naturally and supernaturally. He urged all women to be active politically and socially insofar as such activity would not interfere with their primary duties as wives and mothers.

Pius XII saw the dangers and advantages of automation before anyone, except perhaps American unions. While he warned against the dangers of the depersonalization of society and the unemployment of many workers because of automation, he considered it essentially good for increasing production, lowering the cost of goods and services, and freeing men from many routine and burdensome jobs. "Would we be reasonable or even Christian to shackle the future," he asked, "by holding it back? The church, on the contrary, asks the faithful to see in the astounding progress of science the realization of the plan of God, who has entrusted to man the discovery and exploitation of the wealth of the universe." The Pope requested industry, unions, and government to devise ways to cushion the shock of the displaced worker and prepare him for other employment.

Most Catholics were affected more directly by the liturgical changes he authorized than by his other measures of adaptation to a changing world. His were the first breakthroughs in an antiquated and largely meaningless liturgy: the easing of fasting regulations for a no longer rural populace, the permission for evening Mass, the use of one's native language for part of the rites in administering some sacraments, active lay participation in the Mass on a limited scale, and a drastic revision of the Holy Week services — radical innovations for the conservatives of the time.

Like Paul VI and John XXIII, Pius XII pulled back when the flow of progress, in his view, threatened to become a torrent. In 1950 he reasserted traditional teaching on infallibility by solemnly proclaiming the Assumption and he published *Humani Generis,* in which he urged theologians and Scripture scholars to "engage in most careful research, but with the necessary prudence and caution."

Pius XII was not impetuous about change. He was conservative in wanting to preserve sound tradition, but the consistent theme of his pontificate was to adapt that tradition to a changing world. His early moves to make the church relevant to today's world, and especially his two challenging encyclicals *Mediator Dei* and *Mystici Corporis* made possible Vatican II and the work of his successors John XXIII and Paul VI. His intellectual breakthrough will eventually be perhaps more important, though less engaging, than John's emotional breakthrough.

2. The Practicality of "Idealism"

During his long pontificate Pope Pius XII repeatedly treated the problem of peace in his Christmas messages and occasional other letters and allocutions. These constitute the most profound consideration on the nature and requirements of peace in modern times. They were respectfully received by most people in the free world, but generally dismissed as impractical theorizing about the nature of peace instead of getting down to the practical problem of how to attain it.

The difficulty in finding a way to initiate and conduct discussions on ending the war in Vietnam suggests that Pius XII was eminently practical, and that if his advice could have been followed the problems confronting statesmen today would not be as difficult as they are.

In his 1940 Christmas message Pius XII listed five "victories" needed as preliminaries to any lasting peace. One of these is victory over distrust which makes honest understanding between governments impossible. Victory over mutual distrust and suspicion is almost impossible to achieve in today's world and it will certainly not be won until statesmen consistently match their words with their deeds.

When Goldberg tells the UN how anxious we are to negotiate a peace in Vietnam and on the same day McNamara tells reporters that he is placing an order for 280 more fighter-bombers into 1968, the rest of the world is hardly induced to trust our peaceful intentions.

Trust must be mutual, of course, and there is nothing that we can do directly to make the governments of Hanoi, Peking, and

Moscow trustworthy. The most we can do to initiate a victory
over mistrust among nations is to see that our deeds do not belie
our words. This might be a beginning toward a victory over mistrust. It is the only beginning we can make. Propaganda propa-
gates mistrust, and every government has its propaganda machine.

Pius XII defined peace as "tranquil living together in order."
Peace is primarily a spiritual and moral condition. It is, he insisted,
a threefold thing, and no one aspect of it can be attained permanently without the other two. It is first of all an interior state
of soul and condition of mind within each person; second, it is
a domestic matter within each nation, social peace among the
classes within the nation: and third, it is a tranquil living together in order by the nations of the world.

This might sound highly theoretical, an analysis of peace that
has no connection with treaties and sanctions against aggression.
But we can understand its practical reality when we read the
utterances and see the faces of people with whom the President
seeks to find a consensus. Few exhibit tranquility of mind and
soul.

Again, one need only listen to Hawks screech at Doves to see
how Pius' analysis is far from mere theory, or how our domestic
racial troubles and neglected pockets of poverty at home destroy
our image as a nation that desires to protect human freedom and
lead other peoples to lands of bounty throughout the world.
Violence and riots in our streets, brought into our homes on
radio and TV, are not conducive to the social peace and tranquility of mind that people in a democracy must have to pursue
intelligently international peace.

A glance at today's embroiled world and our dilemma on
foreign policy shows how soundly Pius spoke in his Christmas
Eve message of 1942. "Internation relations and internal order
are intimately related. International equilibrium and harmony
depend on the internal equilibrium and development of the individual States in the material, social, and intellectual spheres. A
firm and steady peace policy toward other nations is in fact impossible without a spirit of peace within the nation which in-

spires trust. It is only then, by striving for an internal peace, a peace in both fields, that people will be freed from the cruel nightmare of war."

All will admit that we can do more than we have to establish social peace in our land. But what about other nations, the Vietnams, Indonesias, and Congos? Here again we might consider another of Pius XII's necessary preconditions of lasting peace. It is impossible, he wrote, to have peace when some nations remain impoverished and are denied access to natural resources monopolized by the rich nations. But Congress consistently appropriates more than the President requests for military purposes and less than he requests for nonmilitary foreign aid, and now for his war on poverty — apparently because this is how they read their constituencies.

The Pope's formula, in effect, was more bread and fewer bullets; Congress' has been less bread and more bullets. I wonder whether Congress is more realistic than Pius XII was. So far in this century we have not shot our way into a true and lasting peace anywhere.

Pius XII frequently called for an international institution with power to enforce agreements among nations. This sounds much more realistic as a means for maintaining peace than a United Nations that is not allowed to be much more than a world forum, valuable as that function might be.

This leads to the consideration that Pope Paul's *Matri Christi* might be looked on as the letter of a diplomatic realist rather than merely a pietistic call to say the rosary for the intention of peace during the month of the rosary. True, that is the call. But it is not like the call to say a liturgically inappropriate rosary at a wake. The encyclical is charged with emotion, as well it should be at this juncture of world affairs. But the appeal is to reason, an appeal not to escalate the conflict in Vietnam or tensions elsewhere, an appeal to "work out concrete plans and terms in all sincerity."

The appeal is eminently practical, even though in this time of mutual mistrust and suspicion it might seem to many to be idealistic and unreal. What can be more practical than to insist that "peace must rest on justice and the liberty of mankind and take into account the rights of individuals and communities. Otherwise, it must be shifting and unstable." Finally, as long as men do everything humanly possible to work for true peace, what can be more practical than to pray to Him who is the "Prince of Peace"?

3. Humanism Joins the Church

Pope Paul VI put his encyclical *Populorum Progressio* in the tradition of *Rerum Novarum, Quadragesimo Anno, Mater et Magistra,* and *Pacem in Terris.* It develops the social teaching of these great encyclicals by applying it to changing social, economic, and political conditions, and by giving this teaching a humanistic rather than moralistic and legalistic cast.

Thus far it has not been given the balanced analysis it deserves, partly, I suspect, because it was published under 87 titled subheadings which tempted news analysts to read only the paragraphs that seemed to be newsworthy. As a result, scant attention was given to what will be the most important part of *Populorum Progressio.*

The section of this encyclical which will have the most important and lasting relevance is that in which Paul states the church's social teaching in terms of Christian humanism. Significantly, this encyclical was written in French and frequently cites French sources. Thus it moves from the Roman legalistic view of social matters, a just wage, a fair profit, and so on, to the French humanism of such men as Jacques Maritain and Henri de Lubac. *Rerum Novarum* and *Quadragesimo Anno* considered the social question in European terms, whereas John XXIII studied it in global and universalist terms. Like John's *Pacem in Terris, Populorum Progressio* is addressed to "all men of good will" and it is global in its vision.

"Today," Paul wrote, "the principal fact that we must all recognize is that the social question has become world-wide." Thus the church must take "a global vision of man and of the human race." Such a vision reveals an enormous imbalance be-

between the few nations who enjoy great wealth and the world's
many hungry peoples. The concern of this encyclical is the ad-
vancement of the poor and hungry peoples to full human
development materially, intellectually, and spiritually.

The heart of the encyclical is the section on the "Christian
Vision of Development." Here Paul tells us that he is concerned
with each man, each group, the whole of humanity, each person
of mankind having a vocation which he must fulfill completely.
The church and governments in both developed and underdeveloped countries have the obligation of making it possible for
every man to develop his potential completely, to realize his complete self-fulfillment.

"This self-fulfillment is not something optional. Just as the
whole of creation is ordained to its Creator, so spiritual beings
should of their own accord orientate their lives to God. . . . This
harmonious enrichment of nature by personal and responsible
effort is ordered to a further perfection. By reason of his union
with Christ, the source of life, man attains to new fulfillment
of himself, to a transcendent humanism which gives him his
greatest possible perfection: this is the highest goal of personal
development."

The development of peoples must go through stages from "less
human conditions" to "conditions that are more human" to "conditions that are still more human." These advances involve such
achievements as the possession of material necessities, the growth
of knowledge, and the acquisition of culture. "Basic education,"
the Pope writes, "is the primary object of any plan of development . . . an illiterate is a person with an undernourished mind."

Such a statement typifies the development of the church's social
doctrine since Vatican II. The conclusion of the first part of
Populorum Progressio tells us: "What must be aimed at is complete humanism. And what is that if not the fully-rounded development of the whole man and of all men? . . . True, man
can organize the world apart from God, but 'without God can
organize it in the end only to man's detriment.' [quoting De
Lubac]. There is no true humanism but that which is open to

the Absolute and is conscious of a vocation which gives human life its true meaning."

Paul condemns the old laissez-faire capitalism, an economy regulated by absolutely free competition with each competitor morally uninhibited in his pursuit of profit. This, certainly, does not describe the mixed economy of any developed country in the world today. The Pope also points out that free trade between developed and underdeveloped countries puts the latter at a disadvantage and makes their development almost impossible.

The most shocking paragraphs to most Americans, however, are the blunt statements of Catholic social teaching as old as the New Testament. The Pope calls upon individuals and nations to support undertakings to end hunger and destitution suffered by their neighbors. "To them," and Paul uses strong words, "we could apply also the parable of the rich man whose fields yielded an abundant harvest and who did not know where to store his harvest: "God said to him: 'Fool, this night do they demand your soul of you.' "

In the second part of this encyclical the Pope strikes a note of urgency. "Let everyone be convinced of this: the very life of poor nations, civil peace in developing countries, and world peace itself are at stake." This calls for a new orientation in the battle for world peace.

The enemy now is not the Communism of old, but the hunger destitution, and frustration of the underdeveloped parts of the world. All men of goodwill, he concludes, must be committed to "the struggle against underdevelopment." The "hour for action has now sounded," and "the new name for peace is development."

Populorum Progressio will most likely go down in history not only for shifting the church's social teaching from a moralistic to a humanistic basis, but also for shifting the attack from one against a Communism that has disintegrated intellectually and politically to one against the new enemy of hunger, poverty, and subhuman conditions under which most of the world lives and which is now the most formidable threat to world peace.

4. U. S. Bishops and Nationalism

Most Catholics take justifiable pride in their church's role in social matters, such as the tardy but sincere identification of most of the hierarchy with the civil rights movement and the earlier commitment to decent wages for the workingman. These are cases of authentic implementation of Catholic social and moral teaching. One stance of the hierarchy, however, which is a cause of embarrassment to many thinking Catholics is its position or lack of position on the war in Vietnam.

Except for isolated statements of individual bishops there is little on the record.

In his annual Christmas visit to troops in Vietnam in 1965, the late Cardinal Spellman said of his country, "I fully support everything it does." And in answer to reporters' questions he repeated Stephan Decatur's famous aphorism: "My country, may it always be right. Right or wrong, my country." These words are embarrassing. They could have been uttered by a patriotic American in the warmth of speechmaking, as Decatur originally phrased them in a toast. But the Cardinal never modified them later, and he repeated them in 1966.

Cardinal Spellman was more extremely nationalistic than other bishops, but their rare mentions of our position in Vietnam do not suggest any serious reexamination of what we are doing there. Mostly, the American bishops have been thunderingly silent about our activity in Vietnam, and either refuse or neglect to participate with other Christians in urging the Administration to take all possible steps to move into peace negotiations. This is the only major issue in recent times on which American bishops have not supported the papal approach. How can we explain this phenomenon? Why do American bishops, so loyal to Rome in other respects, put American foreign policy beyond judgment?

From the very beginning of our national history most bishops have tried to demonstrate by word and deed that Catholics consider loyalty one of the most important virtues. With a few outstanding exceptions, like Bishop John Spalding of Peoria, they seem never to have thought that there might sometimes be conflict between loyalty to country and loyalty to truth or to God. They have consistently sought to show how American the church is and how missionary America is. They have, with few exceptions, held America above criticism — except, of course, in matters of sexual morality.

Americans are not the only super-patriots in the church. In an age of nationalism, Catholics have been in the forefront against socialism, Communism, naturalism, and other "secular heresies," but they identified with nationalism in a simplistic way that now embarrasses the historian, mostly, I believe, because almost everywhere they felt themselves under suspicion of divided allegiance.

The Action Française, perfervid in its hatred against Jews and Germans, attracted notable Catholics in France before it was condemned by Rome. Poles deified their country as "the Christ of the nations" that had redeemed other nations by its partitioning and would arise again on the third day. Irishmen identified Catholicism and nationalism against England, as most Italian Catholic leaders warmly endorsed Fascism and Mussolini's invasion of Ethiopia, and Spanish Catholics followed Franco as a modern El Cid.

This superpatriotism was understandable in the past. It is a thing of the past among most leaders of the church in Europe, as it is among most secular statesmen. But it hangs on here embarrassingly. Perhaps a partial explanation is that American statesmen still speak in tongues of pre-war superpatriotism, never doubting that we are on the side of God in all our endeavors and Catholic leaders are still captivated by that same conviction. Such an explanation excuses them from meaningful membership in the whole People of God in favor of a more meaningful membership in the American nation and a refusal to judge America by Christian norms — except for sexual morality.

Dorothy Dohen's *Nationalism and American Catholicism* shows how and why a man like Cardinal Spellman can be so superpatriotic. He is the victim of a heritage that he simplisticly accepts as being loyal Americanism and sound Catholicism. In her study Dorothy Dohen examines the writings and speeches of Bishops Carroll, England, Hughes, Ireland, Gibbons, and Spellman, using the more intellectual Bishop Spalding as a "control." Professor Dohen shows how Archbishop Carroll assumed the compatibility of American government and Catholicism, and how his successors were pushed by circumstances to profess their Americanism in ever more strident tones.

Hers is a fully documented sociological study which seeks to explain rather than condemn. It shows how the nativist reaction to Catholic immigrants speaking foreign tongues drove Catholic leaders to overstress how really American were these Catholics because of their religion, which blossomed fully in the clime of American democracy. It explains how men like Ireland saw the danger of a nationally fragmented church in this country if Germans and other non-English-speaking Catholics did not enter into the mainstream of America. Thus they warned against foreign nationalisms while succumbing to American nationalism.

Perhaps it was inevitable in their adapting the church to American society that the bishops should speak as superpatriots. One can understand the flamboyant Ireland writing over sixty years ago: "With our hopes are bound up the hopes of the millions of the earth. The church triumphing in America, Catholic truth will travel on the wings of American influence, and encircle the universe. . . . I have called America the providential nation. Even as I believe that God rules over men and nations, so do I believe that a divine mission has been assigned to the Republic of the United States. That mission is to prepare the world, by example and moral influence, for the universal reign of human liberty and human rights. America does not live for herself alone; the destinies of humanity are in her keeping." Understandable in 1905, perhaps, but do these words sound authentically Christian after Vatican II?

How much more authentic are the words of Bishop Spalding written about the same time: "There is a higher love than love of country — the love of truth, the love of justice, the love of righteousness; and he alone is a patriot who is willing to suffer obloquy and the loss of money and friends, rather than betray the cause of truth, justice, and righteousness, for only by being faithful to this can he rightly serve his country."

5. God Becomes a Slogan in Modern Holy Wars

Many years ago Hilaire Belloc wrote that all wars are, at bottom, theological. Most historians would consider this too sweeping an assertion, since many wars have been for limited objectives — such as rounding off a boundary line — and they were fought with proportionately limited manpower and finances. Only a war that is at bottom theological justifies unlimited investment of lives, weapons, careers, and finances, and requires total victory. Both of the great world wars were theological, as was our Korean war, our war in Vietnam, and the six-day war in the Middle East.

This is the fundamental reason why negotiations appear frustrating to outsiders who are not committed to total victory for one side or the other. Canadians, Britishers, Frenchmen, and others cannot understand Washington's position on the Vietnam war, nor can we really understand the total victory goal of either the Israeli or the Arabs in their "holy war."

Belloc's thesis throws light on the puzzle of Vietnam doves becoming pro-Israel hawks, and Vietnam hawks becoming dove-like on the Israeli-Arab war. One tends to be hawk or dove according to whether one is fighting for his God — secularized now of course, under such names as nationalism, liberty, human rights, the containment of Communism, or the liberation of people from the tyranny of totalitarian rule. Belloc's almost forgotten thesis also helps explain why various polls have found Christians and Jews ranking among the least militaristic of all on Vietnam and the most militaristic on the recent Israeli-Arab war.

Along with many excellent traditions and norms, Christians of the New Testament inherited from Jews of the Old Testament the idea that their God was a God of battle, that the Chosen People would eventually triumph when their God helped them strike down the last of His and their enemies. Most Jewish leaders, because of historical circumstances, elected to stress Jewish nationalism and ignore the universalism to which some prophets called the Chosen People. Christians and Moslems became universalists, but they cultivated the militarism they had inherited from the Jews. Thus, ironically, the three peoples having "a religion with a book" continued to consider war theologically.

As there was tension between universalism and nationalism among the Jews, so among Christians there has always been tension between the militaristic inheritance of the Old Testament and Christ's call to put down the sword. In the first centuries Christians were not militaristic, and many of them were complete pacifists. But when they found themselves nearly encircled by a crescent of Moslems from Syria to Spain, they undertook the militarily foolish but (to their way of thinking) theologically sound crusades. The resounding call to arms by Pope Urban II, in which he also offered many material and sensual inducements, was answered by the cry "God wills it!" and the crusades were under way.

There were great deeds of valor; many legends interlacing religion and violence were created; even a pathetic crusade of unarmed children glorified God by scattering their bones across the sands of North Africa. The reluctant crusader, the skeptic Frederick II, who was excommunicated for not starting on time, secured more by negotiation than any of the crusades except the first. Nevertheless, Frederick was denounced by theologians for his willingness to deal with the heretic rather than kill him.

Meanwhile, medieval Christian theologians developed a set of conditions for a "just war," and the church limited fighting in various ways. Thus an ambiguous legacy was bequeathed to Christians as they emerged from the Middle Ages with a legacy personified by the armored St. George on horseback and barefooted

St. Francis of Assisi unconvincingly amalgamated in Sir Galahad of the Round Table. St. George prevailed in modern times, not only among Catholics but among most other Christians who believed they were obliged to fight for the honor of their God. Thus the "Politiques," Catholics who believed the religious wars of the sixteenth century in France could be ended by negotiation, were condemned as men "who prefer the repose of the kingdom to the salvation of their souls, who would rather the kingdom remain at peace without God than at war for Him."

On a more spiritual level, the ex-soldier Ignatius Loyola called upon his followers to enlist in God's army. His "Spiritual Exercises" became the most widely used schema for lay as well as clergy retreats. Its climactic moment was when the retreatant decided, after meditating on God's army and the devil's, to enlist in the army of righteousness and to go into the world to fight against the devil and all his works.

The cause was good, of course, and the spirit was militaristic. But where did one find Christ, except as a general?

Catholics and other Christians, suspected of double allegiance, vied with each other to be ultrapatriotic in supporting the national states that came into being in modern times. Catholics were generally among the most nationalistic supporters of their states and their international wars. Those who questioned the justness of any war were few in number, and they were dismissed as eccentrics, as cowards, or as bad Catholics.

Thus the unfolding of history in Western Civilization made Christians, especially Catholics, predisposed to see each war as just, as a defense of their God and their Christian way of life. Meanwhile, the Arabs had lost their ardor for Mohammed's "Jihad" or holy war. But when they were touched by Western Civilization after centuries of somnambulance and they awakened to enter the stream of history again, they revived the doctrine of the holy war as a means of taking what they considered their rightful place in the world.

Still another concept of holy war developed among the Communists, who believed they were fighting against the evil of capitalism and for a future perfect society without violence or injustice.

Thus today wars are almost bound to be "holy wars," as more and more states are developing arsenals that can obliterate their evil enemies — and perhaps, in retaliation, themselves and the rest of the world. Holy wars were destructive enough when the means of killing and destroying were limited. Now they can be totally destructive.

Perhaps for the sake of survival, it is time to adopt the attitude of Frederick II and the French "Politiques." Even more, is it not time to inquire how one best serves his God and fights for His causes?

6. *The Credibility Gap in Church and State*

Deep concern about the "credibility gap" is still another indication that we are rapidly moving into a new society. The important thing from an historian's point of view is not so much that there is a credibility gap as that it should be a matter of stirring concern and even shock to most people. This implies that we expect candor and absolute full truth on the part of statesmen in both church and state. And this is something new.

In days past only commanders of armies reported on battles — and no one seemed to be overly concerned that there was seldom a loser and usually two winners of each battle. The first time that reporters and photographers were on the scene of battle was in the Crimean War in the mid-nineteenth century. The result of their stories and pictures was a complete reorganization of the incredibly inefficient English war department.

But this did not lead to candor on the part of government spokesmen or primary interest in the full objective truth on the part of most newsmen. Atrocity stories abounded during World War I, for example, and because they were sensational few newsmen rejected them, and few readers doubted them. In World War II sophisticated people were more amused than indignant that General Patton's reports on German soldiers he captured began to approach the number of the entire German army. This was expected of such an eccentric but successful general.

Moreover, governments were expected to "manage the news." This meant that they were understood to give their version of events, to suppress part of the truth, to give their side of the story much as a prosecuting attorney or a defense lawyer gave only one side of a case.

But now we are in a new age, when candor and the full, precise truth are demanded of statesmen in both church and state. Such demands have pressured statesmen and churchmen, as well as such others as automobile manufacturers, into making premature and not entirely truthful statements. Sometimes they are speaking out of unadmitted ignorance, sometimes intentionally to deceive.

The Warren Report on President Kennedy's assassination is a typical statement that lacks full and absolute credibility. The almost countless denials of civilian casualties in Vietnam, and then their minimization when they could no longer be denied, are more examples. Statements from religious superiors are sometimes also incredible. This can also be said of government and business spokesmen.

Statesmen and churchmen should realize that technologically and psychologically we are in a new age. Improved communications media make it more difficult to conceal or contort the truth for any length of time, and people insist as never before on their right to know. For these reasons, the long accepted practice of issuing statements that were not quite true or were not true at all is no longer accepted. And when such statements are issued, they are soon found to be false. Then, like the boy who cried "wolf" too often, government officials are not believed when they do make a true statement. It is getting so that executives in church, state, and business can no longer resign "for reasons of health." People demand to know why they were fired. This is the credibility gap.

It is difficult to draw a line between the people's right to know and the harm that releasing information might do to foreign policy, the conduct of a war, and even to persons' lives and reputations. The line is drawn by government authorities and chancery offices. Naturally they draw the line in favor of secrecy and against the public's right to know. Newsmen have the job of seeing that the line is drawn as much in the other direction as possible.

Secrecy is one thing, and under certain conditions it is justifiable. Falsehood is another thing. One cannot justify the contention of Arthur Sylvester, spokesman for the Department of Defense for almost six years, that a government has the right to mislead the public on occasion. This is not to insist on the candor which requires a young man to say exactly what he thinks of his girl friend's new hat. There are generally accepted evasions that no one used to take literally: "I resigned for reasons of health," or "We would love to take the puppy, but John's allergy can't tolerate dogs." These little evasions create no credibility gap because they are not taken literally. But one who repeatedly uses even the little evasion gets the reputation of being a liar.

This is why the late Msgr. J. D. Conway said that "the chancery office is the last place from which you can expect the full truth." This is why every statement made by spokesmen of the Johnson Administration is now suspect. How much more confidence we would have in government statements about the war in Vietnam today if in the past its spokesmen had admitted they might be killing civilians in North Vietnam, or even admitted that they didn't really know. Why not exploit the long range advantage of being credible? The truth emerges sooner than it used to, causing the credibility gap to occur sooner and become wider.

Hanoi is no more credible than Washington, usually even less so. But Hanoi has a theoretical subjective justification we do not enjoy. Marxian theory holds that truth is relative, that news and education are weapons to be used in the class struggle, that there is no difference between them and propaganda. Their evasions, their management of the news, their falsehoods thereby become for them philosophically as well as tactically true. No such defense can be employed by us who believe in objective truth. We should admit that we are lying when we are.

Apart from the morality of the matter why not exploit telling the truth? The first truth uttered freely, and not as the result of exposure of a past lie, will not be believed. But as one verifiable truth follows another, the credibility gap will begin to close. Classified information is justifiable. Security under certain conditions, yes; management of the news to mislead the public, no.

7. Chanceries Should Conduct Their Own Surveys

The *Pastoral Constitution on the Church in the Modern World* tells us that the church learns and profits from progress in the sciences and other secular accomplishments. The poll conducted on how Catholics view their church for *Newsweek* recently is the most dramatic unrequested contribution of data supplied by the secular word to American readers, including bishops and chancery officials.

It is somewhat ironic that chancery offices have not been conducting questionnaires themselves, and find themselves getting data (wanted or not, good and/or bad) from a secular poll. The Harris poll, which I have not seen, may have asked some wrong questions, not asked right ones, and phrased some questions poorly. Nevertheless, it was an attempt to use a scientifically constructed questionnaire to find out how Catholics view their church.

Little such work has been done by church officials. Thus the irony that consultation of the faithful on a wide scale had to be done by an extra-ecclesiastical agency for a secular magazine. Many bishops and chancery officials believe they know pretty well what their faithful think, what they need, what their problems are. The fact is that they know this only of the vocal few.

The rebels are visible and audible. So are the reactionaries. But both are small in number, and they give bishops and all the rest of us a contorted view of the faithful. Only well-constructed questionnaires can give an accurate view. And they must be by interview, because extremists or those intensely involved mail back questionnaires in disproportionate numbers as compared to the secure or indifferent. Apathy is not discovered by return mail.

Why not computerize the chancery? There is nothing necessarily inhuman about this, and it even seems necessary to carry out both the spirit and the letter of Vatican II. The bishop is ruler, leader, teacher, and sanctifier of his diocese. He is also, in some sense, representative of the People of God under his jurisdiction. Infallible declarations on the Immaculate Conception and the Assumption were inaugurated when many bishops petitioned the pope to make such a statement. Pius IX and Pius XII then consulted not only with theologians and Scripture scholars, but also with many more bishops. Implicit in their statements as chief teachers and representatives of their respective dioceses was that this was what the people of the diocese also believed or desired.

If bishops are to reflect accurately the needs, attitudes, beliefs, and practices of their faithful, it is remiss to do so by hunch when adequate research techniques are available. Vatican II advises in the *Decree Concerning the Pastoral Office of Bishops in the Church* that in consulting about the welfare of the faithful the bishops should "employ suitable methods, especially social research." And the *Pastoral Constitution on the Church in the Modern World* tells pastors to make use "especially of psychology and sociology."

It would be wrong, of course, to go so far as Rousseau or Lamennais to equate the voice of the people, the "general will" expressed by the majority, with infallibility, or to think that bishops should equate public opinion with true doctrine. Doctrine is hardly to be found by Gallup or Harris polls.

But it is equally wrong to ignore the faithful on questions of doctrine, as well as attitude, opinion, and practice. In *The Dogmatic Constitution on the Church* Vatican II stated: "The body of the faithful as a whole, anointed as they are by the Holy One, cannot err in matters of belief. Thanks to a supernatural sense of the faith which characterizes the people as a whole, it manifests this unerring quality when, from the bishops down to the last member of the laity, it shows universal agreement in matters of faith and morals."

Such an expression of infallibility is certainly more acceptable to many Protestants than the popularly held one of the Pope alone expressing infallible teaching when he speaks *ex cathedra* on his own on a matter of faith or morals. This, of course, was a favorite theme of Newman, and it does not in any way limit the authoritative teaching power of the bishops and Pope.

Both the controlling ideas and the explicit statements of Vatican II tell us that God reveals Himself in some measure and in various ways in all members of the People of God. "Christ, the great Prophet, who proclaimed the kingdom of His Father by the testimony of His life and the power of His words, continually fulfills His prophetic office until His full glory is revealed. He does this not only through the hierarchy who teach in His name and with His authority, but also through the laity."

Later in the same document we are told: "An individual layman, by reason of the knowledge, competence, or outstanding ability which he may enjoy is permitted and sometimes even obliged to express his opinion on things which concern the good of the church. When occasions arise, let this be done through the agencies set up by the church for this purpose." What agencies now exist in most dioceses? How many of the faithful feel free to express their minds to their bishops or his associates in the chancery? How many bishops are predisposed to listen to any but prestigious laymen in the spirit of these words of Vatican II? What better way is available for finding how Christ "fulfills His prophetic office . . . also through the laity" than by consulting them through scientifically constructed questionnaires?

In the *Pastoral Constitution on the Church in the Modern World* the council Fathers explain that each nation must learn how to "express Christ's message in its own way." They continue with this significant paragraph: ". . . the church requires special help, particularly in our day, when things are changing very rapidly and the ways of thinking are exceedingly various. She must rely on those who live in the world, are versed in different institutions and specialties, and grasp their innermost significance in the eyes of both believers and unbelievers. With the help of the Holy Spirit, it is the task of the entire People of God, especially pastors and theologians, to hear, distinguish, and interpret the many voices of our age, and to judge them in the light of the divine Word. In this way, revealed truth can always be more deeply penetrated, better understood, and set forth to greater advantage."

To do this, it seems to me, the bishops must consult the faithful through frequent questionnaires. This would operate on different levels of belief and opinion. How better to ascertain how God reveals Himself in some way in all persons made to His image? How better to get an accurate view of the attitudes, the needs, the desires of most of the faithful on specific problems confronting the church in various nations and dioceses? Computerize the chancery? How else follow the directives of the bishops assembled in Vatican Council II?

8. Lay Boards Were Inevitable

Vesting independent boards of trustees with ownership and control of Catholic colleges and universities hitherto owned by religious orders is practically inevitable if these colleges and universities are to survive. It is also a healthy development. But it creates some baffling problems which only time and experience will resolve. One of these problems is the academic tenure of members of the religious orders which owned these institutions.

Academic tenure is essential for safeguarding the professor's freedom in research and teaching. There is normally a trial period of about seven years, during which time a teacher can be dismissed on sufficient notice. If he is retained after this trial period, he has permanent tenure and can be dismissed only for grave reasons spelled out in his contract and generally accepted by the academic community. Typical of these grave reasons are notorious public scandal, or lack of productive scholarship.

Members of religious orders were customarily appointed to a college or university position by their superior, and the institution automatically accepted the appointee. This quite unacademic arrangement was not always as bad as it might have been, because university trustees — themselves members of the religious order — and the religious superior often cooperated in planning the education and the placement of religious in various teaching and administrative positions.

Religious without academic qualifications were sometimes assigned by their superiors to academic positions, and they became another "cross" the institution had to bear. Occasionally, too, brilliant religious professors were jerked out of academic life by their superiors, perhaps because the superior felt the professors were becoming proud, attracting too much attention, were too controversial, or embarrassingly honest.

Academic tenure, which at least some Catholic universities accorded their lay professors, was thus denied to religious professors. This is harmful to the institution as well as the individual priest- or nun-professor. One of the difficult problems facing the new independent boards of trustees, then, is to develop a sound plan of academic tenure for these religious professors.

Presuming that they will be truly interested in the academic excellence of their institutions, the new boards of trustees must work out norms on the appointment, promotion or dismissal, and security of tenure of religious professors. Who is to take the initiative in appointing a religious to an academic position? His religious superior? The interested department or college in the university? This is similar to the age-old problem of king and pope in the selection of bishops. Each had to have either appointive or veto power. Obviously, the academic institution must have the right to refuse any religious not qualified to hold an academic or administrative position.

Obviously, too, the religious superior has an obligation to assign his personnel to positions that will best achieve the goals of the order and the welfare of the individual religious. If a Jesuit or a Holy Cross priest, for example, expresses an interest in sociology, becomes well trained in that discipline and is therefore academically qualified, must the college or university accept him? What if it does not need him? From the standpoint of academic excellence, the institution should not have to accept him and pay him the going salary when there is no vacancy for him.

There is bound to be a trial-and-error period during which the needs of the university and those of the religious order are somehow coordinated. This seems to require closer cooperation between the two than often existed when the order owned the college or university, but when its provincial was less interested in academic affairs than in missions or retreats. Matters can hardly be worse than in the past, when academic qualifications were often a secondary consideration in making academic appointments.

The matter of promotion or dismissal should present no real problem. Priest- or nun-professors would be promoted according to the same criteria used for other professors and generally accepted by the academic community — productive scholarship, participation in the academic life of the institution, and good teaching.

The matter of permanent academic tenure, however, is a serious problem. This has been frequently violated in the past, and unless sound policy is formulated by the new boards of trustees it will continue to be violated in the future. Some Catholic colleges and universities have worked out good arrangements on academic tenure which protect professors in their academic freedom from administrators and boards of trustees alike. Religious professors can be similarly protected without any problem. But what about protection from their religious superiors? This is the real problem.

It seems to me that members of religious orders (who will be paid salaries according to rank and competence) will have to be engaged under somewhat different tenure. The usual contract between an academic institution and a teacher lists causes of dismissal, such as public scandal, and spells out procedures that the institution must follow in stating causes and providing hearings on them. Some special contract seems needed for religious, perhaps providing for him to maintain security of tenure as long as he is a priest (or she a nun) in good standing in the religious order. This would protect religious who become properly laicized, but not those who "go over the hill" and show up with a spouse. There may be other special provisions for the tenure of religious professors which discussion between new boards of trustees and religious superiors will evolve.

The academic institution can hardly expect religious superiors to release all hold over their priests or nuns when they become professors. Perhaps times can be worked out — six years seems to be the magic number — when the religious superior would be free to reassign a member of his order without violating his academic tenure. Consultation beforehand would enable the institution to plan to replace the individual, just as enforced retirement of lay professors can be foreseen and planned for.

At any rate, this is a problem to which religious orders and the new boards of trustees must give their attention in days to come. How to resolve this problem consonant with norms accepted by the American academic community is the heart of the problem.

9. It's Time to Revamp the Children's Parish

One does not have to travel much to realize that renewal in the church does not come down from on high. Permission must come from above, but renewal comes from the conversion of the individual person and a grass-roots renewal of each parish. There are some lay Traditionalist activists, almost always inspired by a Traditionalist priest. But the words and actions of such activists are enough to sell renewal to most Catholics. The Traditionalists are no threat to renewal.

If it is possible to pinpoint the real obstacle to renewal (after those bishops who will not permit it), it is the pastor who quietly but stubbornly maintains his pre-Vatican II stance. Not even the Holy Ghost is going to be called Holy Spirit in such a pastor's prayers or parish. The people don't want these changes, he will tell you; they'll quit coming to Mass. Somehow, he believes, this fad will also pass away and the "real Catholic Church" will survive.

God in His wisdom has arranged for the eventual removal of all such pastors. But there are many of the laity who want to experience renewal before that day. They look at parishes where formerly reluctant laymen are enthusiastic about renewal after having experienced at least its beginnings. Trapped in the geographic confines of a benighted block of the church, they favor getting together with like-minded Catholics to form parishes based on something other than geographic lines.

The argument of such people is persuasive. The geographic parish, they explain, was a normal and proper arrangement when

111

families lived generation after generation in the same locale. Those who lived in geographic proximity formed a true community of people who knew each other, who lived together, worshiped together, and were truly concerned about each other. In modern America, however, the turnover in the average metropolitan parish is so great each year that the parish is no more a natural community than the random collection of people on a bus or a train.

I see no objection to forming some experimental parishes, but I believe that the present system has advantages not to be casually surrendered, and most of us should promote renewal in the parish in which we live. To neglect this because of important other commitments in the church's life is something like neglecting one's own family because of time devoted to UNICEF or Brotherhood.

Let us assume that our intransigent pastor has gone to his eternal reward, and with our new pastor we can ask ourselves what to do to make renewal meaningful in our parish. Obviously we opt for fully adopting liturgical changes in all their richness and variety. We soon find ourselves confused. Why not keep the altar rail? It turns out that we willingly accept liturgical renewal without understanding what it is really all about. We soon find that the old catechism is "out," that if we really accept Christ's two commandments of the New Testament, then the Mosaic ten commandments are redundant, legalistic, Old Testament in spirit, and fall far short of forming Christians.

These and other revelations along the line as we move into renewal suggest, perhaps, that our greatest weakness in the parish is its having been exclusively child-oriented. This was proper in the past, perhaps, but is it still the best orientation? In the past Catholics lived in a Protestant culture in which they tried to keep the faith. Parish schools tried to drill religion, both doctrine and practice, into the student so thoroughly that it became a habit he could never break and they were fairly successful. Adults in these parishes were not completely neglected. There were Holy Name societies to put on parades and have beer in the basement instead of the saloon. But adults were important chiefly as supporters of the parish school, as parents concerned with their children's Catholic education, as card party and carnival promoters who raised money for repairs on the church building and enlarging the school. These were good things, but they hardly add up to the fullness of the Christian life.

Is such orientation still necessary? Is it not perhaps an obstacle to real Christian renewal of the parish? Is it necessary that a parish have its own Scout Troop and Cub Pack, its own teams and leagues? Perhaps acceptable, even advisable in certain locales, but not essential. There are advantages to such arrangements. They give the children and their parents an added sense of community — but they leave out most of the other parishioners, who anonymously attend Mass on Sunday and then disappear.

There are some weighty disadvantages in the child-oriented parish. Such parishes tend to maintain religious ghettoes in an age when this is no longer desirable. Another serious disadvantage is that the parish loses a most promising age group, young people in college and several years after graduation who are neither children nor parents. These young people, who potentially have so much to offer, come back into the center of things in the child-oriented parish when their first child enters the parish school. By this time they are involved "mothers" and "fathers" who have missed the vital decade of 16 to 26, when they could have made their continuing contribution to life in the parish, and have now settled down to being protective parents.

The worst disadvantage of the child-oriented parish is that adults are tempted never to mature. Good fathers and mothers are concerned, quite laudably, with their children. They become coaches, den mothers, scout masters, movie makers, and rooters for the teams. This takes time and attention all generously given, some of which might better be given to mature involvement in church renewal. Men and women capable of achieving maturity in the exclusively child-oriented parish continue to be so involved in backing juvenile enterprises that they neglect to become mature.

I do not mean to criticize legitimate concern with children in the parish and with keeping the parish school good in every way. My concern is that in allotting time, energy, and money to the parish we not neglect the continuing development of all of us. None of us was well enough educated formally to understand what the renewal is all about. That learning is a never-ending process is brought home to us forcefully as we try to understand what underlies the changes in liturgical renewal, the meaning of the Eucharistic celebration and the sacraments, where it is that we find Christ, how the Holy Spirit operates, to what extent we can plumb the mystery of God and his church.

Each proposed change in the parish, I therefore suggest, should be studied in the light of whether it will keep the parish simply child-oriented or in some way promote the maturity of all parishioners, children as well as their parents, clerical and religious as well as lay. If renewal is truly to transform a parish, knowledge and understanding of what it is all about and what it involves must be promoted on the grass-roots level. Growth in understanding and commitment is a life-long enterprise.

10. If Rome Understood the Difference in Cultures

Although it is agreed that the *Dogmatic Constitution on the Church* is the basic, most important document issued by Vatican II, the *Pastoral Constitution on the Church in the Modern World* will touch most of us more immediately. It is a bridge, as no other document of Vatican II is, between the church and the world. It is, in many respects, the most radical of the Vatican documents, and the one that has the most direct applicability to us in renewing the church.

Significantly, the *Church in the Modern World* is the only document introduced from the floor of the Council. Cardinal Suenens introduced it, and he was supported by Cardinals Lercaro and Montini in the last days of the first session. It was accepted on the last working day of the Council, and it was addressed "not only to the sons of the Church . . . but to the whole of humanity." It deals with such themes as what the modern world can offer to the church and what the church can give the world, and it is permeated with a humanistic consideration of the dignity of the human person, the excellence of freedom, the autonomy of both the secular and the sacred sciences, and it treats of such matters as war and peace, and social and political life.

One particularly new subject is the chapter on "The Proper Development of Culture." Recent fears about Dutch Catholics expressed in Rome is symptomatic of Rome's failure to understand what the Vatican Fathers said about the church and culture.

Properly to understand the various cultures to which the church must adapt, even more important are the studies of psychiatry and anthropology, both of which are resisted by most Romans as dangerous and even inimical to Catholic doctrine. Thus, accepting this line of reasoning, we reach the impasse of not understanding what the guidelines of this chapter on "The Proper Development of Culture" are all about, because even more than sociology and psychology, psychiatry and anthropology are the key studies to understanding various cultures.

Vatican II's message on this subject is contained in paragraph 59 of the *Church in the Modern World* ". . . culture must be made to bear on the integral perfection of the human person, and on the good of the community and the whole of society. Therefore the human spirit must be cultivated in such a way that there results a growth in its ability to wonder, to understand, to contemplate, to make personal judgments, and to develop a religious, moral, and social sense. Because it flows immediately from man's spiritual and social nature, culture has constant need of a just freedom if it is to develop. It also needs the legitimate possibility of exercising its independence according to its own principles. Rightly, therefore, it demands respect and enjoys a certain inviolability, at least as long as the rights of the individual and of the community, whether particular or universal, are preserved within the context of the common good."

The Vatican Fathers tell us that the church must learn to live in every culture and still transcend them all. Every culture has the right to our respect, whether we like it personally or not. Every culture must develop the person according to its own norms, and it enjoys the right to inviolability "within limits of morality and the general welfare." There are, of course, values and truths which transcend all cultures, such as the right of the individual to his personal dignity and to freedom from discrimination, and on these the church must insist everywhere.

Every major encyclical on the missions since Benedict XV's *Maximum Illud* has instructed missionaries not to identify the church with their own culture, but to adapt it to that of the people among whom they work. Many concessions have been made in the last half century to Asiatic and African ways of life.

But Rome seems to think of cultures as big monolithic units, like Toynbee's 21 civilizations in world history. Thus the Romans fail to realize that the Dutch have different traditions and institutions than do Romans, a point stressed by Cardinal Alfrink when he welcomed the European bishops who met in Holland. To believe that Kansans in Topeka have the same culture as Romans or Neopolitans is to reveal culture blindness.

If culture is a way of life as the Vatican Fathers said, then one must speak of "sub-cultures" to which the church must adapt. It is proper to distinguish the culture of suburbia from the culture of those people condemned to develop poverty as a way of life. It is necessary for lay people, as well as clerics and religious (among whom there are some splendid exceptions) to understand these sub-cultures and to tolerate differences they may find uncomfortable.

This involves the serious problem of not drifting into a cultural relativism which asserts that right and wrong do not transcend cultures but are created by them. Some things, such as the violation of human dignity, transcend cultures. But such matters as the mode of liturgical worship, forms of recreation, art, music, literature, and the like do not.

They should be indigenous to the culture in which they develop, and must be respected as such even in Rome. It is not a matter of bad will on the part of the Romans, but rather lack of culture sensitivity. Somehow it all seems tied in with finding only a vowel difference between the two nouns *urbe* and *orbe*.

11. Looking Upon Our Mother, the Church

Properly enough, there is much concern about young people not having vocations as in the past, about their not attending Mass or receiving the sacraments as they used to, and in general their not staying active within the "institutional church." Religious authorities suggest all sorts of reasons: indifferent parents who do not push vocations, or who do oppose them; sexy movies and pornographic literature; materialistic secularism; the attraction of daring but appealing un-Christian forms of humanism; the resulting "generation gap" between those in authority and the young people who do not listen to them and will not trust them.

There may be something to these alleged reasons, but to dwell on them is to evade consideration of the basic reason for young people not staying with the church, even when, through habit or to placate their elders, they sit in the pew for an hour on Sunday. The basic reason is that the image of the church they were given is false.

It is similar to the shock, though much more traumatic, of a young child who sees his mother in one light day in and day out and then sees her dressed in beautiful formal gown to attend a ball. Unadorned, she is not as shiningly beautiful as she appears leaving for the formal ball. The church has been heavily made-up for centuries, but no one was supposed to know this or admit it. We were taught that anyone who criticized the pope, the curia, the bishop, the chancery, or the pastor was "on the other side" in the struggle between the church and the world, and the devil was speaking through him.

I advert to this matter not because I am saying anything new, but because I think it is a most important fact about the church in our time, and because it does much to explain the disillusionment of a generation led by John Kennedy and John XXIII to expect honesty from their elders. Charles Davis was shocked to discover this dishonesty on his own highly intellectual level — and it drove him out of his Mother's household. In a certain way Davis was as naïve and idealistic as the disillusioned young people in the church. To me and most of us it rather confirmed what we knew all the time: that my mother and my mother-the-church wore makeup in public. My mother, like yours, would readily admit this. The scandal to me and to young Catholics is that churchmen pretend that the church does not wear makeup, that the appearance she presents to the world is an honest, photographic appearance — which, of course, it is not.

Such dishonesty can never be justified. In the past it was accepted and perpetuated by curial and chancery officials on the grounds that this was the only way to "preserve the faith of the faithful," for the myth had to be maintained that those who rose to positions of authority in the church were impeccable, not subject to human weaknesses, and somehow miraculously preserved from making mistakes. Today this pose is harmful to a church which, despite the wishes of curial and chancery officials, has become an open church. All the world can now watch her put on her makeup for public appearances, and we cringe to see what is covered over and, in effect, denied.

Young people have always been impatient with their settled elders. This generation is increasingly impatient because it has become disillusioned with the promises held out a few long years ago. They are not impressed with gradual change, because John XXIII and Vatican II promised radical renewal. They are not impressed with a "youth movement" that replaces an 88-year-old curial official by one only 73. They are not impressed with a dragging liturgical reform that stays safely out of touch with present reality while bishops quibble about guitars. They are not impressed by services that were au courant six centuries ago and are still conducted by princes in medieval finery attended by lesser knights wearing clothes and making obeisance appropriate to that age but distractingly ludicrous today.

These things fail to impress young people, and their elders consider them irreverent. There are other things in the church which distress them: an archbishop's public accusation that one of their favorite scripture scholars is a heretic; the suspicion in which Rome holds many of the new scholars in the church; the flat denial by various bishops and chancery officials that they said what they were heard to say, or the evasive explanation that they did not mean what they said. In short, overt dishonesty by some people placed high in the church shocks and distresses young people. Worst of all, they are shocked to find that documents are sometimes suppressed, altered, occasionally even destroyed, that sometimes truth is not a matter of concern to some church officials.

The first step toward winning the confidence of young people and getting them involved in the life of the church is obviously to admit that churchmen do make mistakes, that investiture into a position of authority does not automatically carry with it impeccability, infallibility, or even charity.

Such an admission would be a move toward closing the honesty gap. But more is required. Bishops and other officials in the church must move quickly and radically to realize the promises held forth in the church by Vatican II.

Older people can cynically shrug off their disappointments about renewal because they never were sure that such promises were meant to be realized. The younger generation, however, believed as children believe. They are becoming traumatically disillusioned, as only children can be. And the only word they hear from many elders in the church is that they must obey and they must respect authority.

PART IV

Toward Peace on Earth

1. DeGaulle Over 76, Is Argument for Forced Retiring at 75

Over a year ago, we wrote: "The mystique of Charles de Gaulle baffles us Americans. How can the leader of a middle-size nation defy the great powers and have them courting his favor? How can he be so popular throughout the world while remaining aloof and almost contemptuous of other statesmen? He is pompous, almost comic, and his grandiose concept of la belle France and himself as a twentieth century Joan of Arc seems ridiculous."

We proceeded to suggest that De Gaulle has been wrong enough, but that he has been right much of the time and that "he has [a year ago] a clearer vision of what is possible in international affairs than do the turmoil-involved leaders of the great powers."

His recent failures, culminating in his pompous, insulting conduct in Canada, require me to modify my previous estimate of his international politics. His consolidating France and liquidating French imperialism remain solid accomplishments. He will be remembered in history for reviving French confidence in their historical destiny.

But his Talleyrand-like maneuvering to represent the small nations of the world in defying the two super-powers of the United States and the U.S.S.R. has not come off. He was not called upon to adjudicate either the Vietnam imbroglio or the Mid-East problem, as he presumed he would be.

And now he has acted more like Citizen Genet than Talleyrand in speaking for a free Quebec, interfering in another country's domestic affairs, speaking to the people against their government, flaunting his popularity with the Quebec extremist minority, and violating not only diplomatic protocol but even good manners in his aborted visit to Canada. This visit was without precedent in international bad manners since the time of De Gaulle's idol, Louis XIV. De Gaulle still puzzles us. His advanced age is part of the explanation, as he seems ever more transfixed by France's and his own past. Like kings and bishops of the past, he is his own first victim, apparently believing that all the world cheers him the way selected crowds listening to his speeches do. He apparently identifies himself with Joan of Arc, Louis XIV, and the two Napoleons who ruled by acclamation and plebiscite and brought France a glory denied to her under more moderate governments.

He was himself apparently puzzled by Prime Minister Lester Pearson's courteous but firm rebuke against him for encouraging Quebec separatism, much as though he did not know that Quebec is not still a French colony and that he was speaking in a federated country known to the rest of us as Canada. Even the French-descended mayor of Montreal had to remind him that Quebec had done well for 200 years without French support or interference. If De Gaulle knew what he was doing in Canada, he cannot be trusted by Frenchmen to conduct their foreign policy; if he did not comprehend what he was doing, he is not competent to head the French government.

De Gaulle's fiasco in Canada revealed the two weaknesses that are more and more warping his judgments: his personal phobia against Britain and America, and the related failure to understand that the world has changed since he was a student reading textbooks about international relations among sovereign national states.

Ever since he was treated as an inconsequential junior partner by Roosevelt and Churchill in the liberation of France and Europe, De Gaulle has nursed a personal resentment that has directed his foreign policy, sometimes for good but increasingly now for the harm of France as well as Britain and the rest of Europe. A case could be made for not receiving Britain into the common market on British terms, but the current exclusion of Britain works a hardship on the countries of the common market, including France.

Perhaps NATO was not needed by 1965 the way it was 20 years earlier, but De Gaulle's brusque unilateral withdrawal did no good except to puff his pride and perhaps that of a France which he seems to consider his mystical body. His hours of ranting against this country when Prime Minister Wilson visited him recently reveal a man no longer rational and objective.

Charles De Gaulle thinks in terms of nationalism, the grandeur of la belle France, the glory of "la patrie." But nationalism is seen by educated people to have been the prime cause of both world wars. For a time it seemed that nationalism was dead except among those who suffered from an educational and cultural time lag. It was repudiated by statesmen and scholars in France and Germany, even to the extent of professors of history in both countries cooperating to revise textbooks cultivating such nationalism. Small irresponsible fringe groups tried to revive nationalism in various European countries, while De Gaulle, as head of state, kindled its smoldering embers in France.

Nationalism is condemned by scholars everywhere, by Pope Paul VI, the World Council of Churches, and most Catholic bishops in all countries but ours. Even in this country only a few members of the hierarchy embrace nationalism with ringing endorsements. De Gaulle has therefore stirred the embers of a fire that was dying and is bound in time to flicker out even among the French peasants. He belongs to the age of the Action Française with its hate-filled slogan "revanche!"

De Gaulle also thinks in outdated terms of balance of power, in which he thinks of nations as neat blocks maneuvered around an international chessboard with each trying to be the one that is decisive in tipping the balance of power in one direction or another. His unavailing attempts to gain that position for France reveal a man empowered to commit his country to a game no longer played in this industrialized world. International sophistication and industrialization have made this outmoded colossus a comic Don Quixote jousting with national windmills that no longer exist.

De Gaulle is, however, over 76. His historical reputation would have been enhanced if France had adopted a compulsory retirement age of 75, for despite his apparent illusion of eternity on earth he displayed advanced senility in his unprecedented diplomatic *faux pas* on his visit to Canada.

2. *Mao Must Accommodate to Survive*

Even Sinologists are not certain of the significance of current happenings in China, simply because no one outside the Bamboo Curtain knows exactly what is happening there. But one does not have to be a Sinologist to see how certain pieces are beginning to fall into place to reveal the standard pattern of history of a country that adopts Marxism-Leninism and tries to put it into practice. Three conclusions, which should help shape our policy on China, seem inescapable.

The first is that Communism simply does not work. Communal ownership of property, as in a religious community or a worker-owned company, is not what I mean by Communism. I mean an ideology, a closed system of thought, which by its very nature is self-defeating when it is put into practice. Lenin was shrewd enough to realize this, and he saved the Soviet revolution in Russia by adopting the NEP (New Economic Policy) in 1921, which accommodated the new Soviet society to many capitalistic devices like incentive pay and private enterprise in the smaller establishments.

Later, when the Russian peasants did not take to the gigantic communal farms and when the starvation and slaughter of millions failed to "convert" them, they were allowed to work their own smaller farms. Thus by ignoring their ideology, Soviet leaders survived. And whenever ideology prevailed over common sense, as in the Lysenko case about the genetics of seed grain, serious losses resulted.

This practical adjustment (so like us) was followed logically by an ideological reassessment and a groping toward a new foreign policy. Thus Russians no longer think only in the closed system of Marxism-Leninism (as Catholic theologians no longer think in a closed system of Aristotelianism). While Soviet thinkers are far from repudiating their Marxism-Leninism, they now study seriously such philosophers as Plato, Teilhard, even Aquinas, all of whom are irrelevant to their system. Soviet foreign policy has also been feeling its way toward adjustment, and this not only because of the rift with China.

Soviet leaders are as anxious as we to reduce defense expenditures so as to put more money into space exploration and consumer goods — and as they do this they are less and less likely to risk a war which can obliterate their accomplishments.

The Soviet pattern is typical rather than unique. It has been followed in the East European countries and more recently in Cuba. Either the original leader must accommodate to a revision of Communist ideology, as well as economic and political policy, or he will be discredited and replaced by one who will. Accommodation in East European countries has brought them a measure of prosperity after years of destitution under rigid Communism. Prosperity seems to make for further accommodation. There seems to be a willingness to make some grudging accommodation to religion, as long as this can be done without completely losing face. Castro has survived by making similar accommodations to reality.

The second conclusion is that this same pattern seems to be working out in China. Mao, like Stalin in the Soviet Union, refuses to accommodate himself and his policies to the hard realities of man and nature. He apparently suffers from the "nemesis of success," for he and his followers achieved power against overwhelming odds and by incredible suffering. His one experience with toleration, when he proclaimed it was time for "a thousand flowers to blossom," sprouted such unexpected weeds of "heresy" that Mao quickly reimposed his rigid Marxist-Leninist ideology.

Reports from China indicate that his principal support comes from students and other young people. This is significant, for these are like young people everywhere who believe that social and political problems can be solved by the simple application of formulas they have learned at school. This generation was born after Mao came to power, and their intellectual diet has been exclusively "the thoughts of Mao Tse-tung."

Opposition to Mao and his rigid policy seems strongest among the workers and the middle-age group. It is led by some high-ranking members of the Communist Party, such as General Secretary Teng Hsiao-ping, army leaders like General Liu Chih-chien, and political figures like President Liu Shao-chi and Vice-Premier Tao Chu. Thus the fight in China takes on the proportions of a civil war.

Obviously, it is to our interest and that of world peace that Mao's opponents succeed. They apparently can accommodate themselves to some kind of coexistence, but with a generation fed nothing but the "thoughts of Mao," his opponents will have to bluster against the "capitalist" nations while modifying his domestic and foreign policies, as Khrushchev had to do.

The third conclusion is that our presence in Vietnam is a great asset for Mao and his followers. Imagine how the Soviet Union's occupation of Cuba or Haiti would strengthen the hawk position in this country and weaken the doves' stand. Imagine how many doves and in-betweeners would be converted into hawks by the Soviet presence in Cuba.

We need only remember how the discovery of Soviet missile sites there incited the temper of this country, and how their removal soothed it. Our presence in Vietnam is a great argument for Mao's maintaining his rigid policy, insisting on complete unity and continued austerity.

Each escalation of the war brings a further confirmation for the Chinese that Mao is right and his opponents are traitors. Each step toward minimizing and ending our involvement in Vietnam is a score for Mao's opponents. Thus our presence in Vietnam is a much bigger thing than Administration spokesmen will admit.

3. A Lesson From History: The Boer War

The British government could not understand why it was condemned as an immoral bully throughout the world during the Boer War (1899–1902). It was even more puzzled that some Englishmen believed the war immoral and sympathized with the Boers. British statesmen believed their cause was right. They had taken the humane step of abolishing slavery throughout the colonies in 1833, and when many of the Boers of South Africa made their "long trek" into the Transvaal rather than give up slaveholding, the British let them go peacefully.

Decades later, when gold and diamonds were found in Boer territory thousands of miners rushed into the Transvaal. Many of them were British citizens — a mark of pride, Lord Palmerston had said, equal to that of the Roman citizen in St. Paul's day. This gold rush was like the ones in California, Colorado, Alaska: rough men seeking a quick fortune, drunk and violent over the weekend, men with no concern for the future of the land, men brazenly defying God's holy law, contemptuous of God's friends tilling the soil.

The righteous Boers taxed these "Uitlanders," or outsiders, unmercifully, and made it difficult for them to acquire citizenship and the vote. Some of the British Uitlanders appealed to their government for protection from these discriminatory practices, as earlier in the century the British had protected citizens supposedly wronged by Greece and by China. The British leaders were puzzled, then, to find themselves accused of being worldwide bullies when they were forced to fight for a just cause, this time on a larger scale and with first-hand coverage of what some complained became a "journalists' war."

Four years earlier the British had created what today we call "a credibility gap," which they never fully understood. Late in 1895 Dr. Jameson rushed British troops into the Transvaal to protect "rioting" Uitlanders. But the Uitlanders had neglected to riot. Jameson's raid was obviously prearranged, and something went wrong with its timing. The Boers and most diplomats were convinced that Cecil Rhodes, prime minister of Cape Colony, had encouraged Jameson, that the colonial office in London knew of the raid in advance and gave it support. Jameson was slapped lightly on his patriotic wrist, and the British government found itself completely innocent.

Somehow this did not convince Boer leaders. When some 21,000 British Uitlanders petitioned the Queen to protect them from political and economic discrimination in the Transvaal, Boer President Kruger proved intractable in negotiations because he righteously knew that God was on his side, and that the British were dissemblers whose real intention was to annex those lands filled with gold and diamonds. Attempts to negotiate the position of the Uitlanders in the Transvaal broke down, and when the British did not accept Kruger's ultimatum to withdraw all troops he declared war.

Back in England this caused little concern. The military, the politicians and the citizenry all underestimated the Boers. Many Boer families had organized the Afrikander Bond, and for two or three years they had been smuggling in arms, chiefly through Delagoa Bay in Portuguese East Africa. Well armed, fighting on their home terrain, motivated by a righteous cause, the Boers decisively routed the British in a series of engagements early in the war.

Now taking the war seriously, the British escalated the conflict, sending in better guns and more men, especially colonials who more easily adapted to the climate and the nature of the Boer War than did the British regulars. Because the Boers were soon overwhelmingly outnumbered, they had to hit and run. In time the war deteriorated into guerilla fighting. The British found it necessary to burn farms near the railroads and other lines of communication. Then they took to burning farms and homes to smoke out guerillas in the interior. The Boer farmer who wanted no part of the war suffered reprisals from both sides. Eventually, the British resorted to ordering all neutrals in certain areas into concentration camps until all Boer guerillas were tracked down.

In this latter part of the war, opposition at home became sharper, and some accusations rang shrill. A "Stop the War Committee" and a "South African Conciliation Committee" were led by respected statesmen. In their propaganda campaign, they exposed the shocking death rate in the concentration camps, organized relief for the inmates, and demanded that civil control replace military control of the camps. The Irish, "long under Britain's heel," sympathized almost to a man with the Boers, even though there were many Irishmen in the British army. Opposition Liberals made conduct of the war a political question, while the Conservative leaders tried to make support of the war a matter of loyalty to the Queen and her glorious Empire.

Accusations and counter-accusations created much heat and even more confusion. Pro-Boers were labelled "Copperheads" who had sympathized with the South in the Civil War. They were also accused of giving aid and comfort to the enemy and of prolonging the war by leading the Boers to believe the English would not carry the war to a conclusion. Papers, such as *The Spectator*, that originally said opposition was essential in a democratic state, came to demand that pro-Boers be silent so that they would no longer influence world opinion and encourage the Boers to continue the war.

Pro-Boers highlighted the burning of farms of families that had taken no part in the war. They stressed the suffering and neglect of children and women in the concentration camps. They pointed out many acts of atrocity, which the severest critics thought added up to a policy rather than mistakes. Many insisted the war was immoral from the very beginning, that it was blatantly an imperialistic war, that British Uitlanders in the Transvaal were hardly exemplary Britishers, and that an immigrant implicitly accepts the laws of the land he enters and the established methods of achieving citizenship and changing the laws.

Eventually this sorry war drew to an end. The Peace of Vereeniging in 1902 provided for a settlement along the pro-Boers' lines. Farmhouses were rebuilt and farms restocked. The Boer states were promised self-government, and within a few years they were brought into the Federation of South Africa as a Dominion in the British Empire. England had also learned that her "splendid isolation" was not so splendid when all the world was against her. She worked out an alliance with Japan shortly before the Boer War ended, and within a few years a quasi-alliance system was worked out with France and Russia.

The British leaders learned what adjustments had to be made as the world turned the calendar page from the nineteenth to the twentieth century. The Boers had lost this sorry war, but the British were intelligent enough to let them win the negotiated Peace of Vereeniging. This gave them their inevitable independence, leaving them friend instead of foe as World War I approached.

4. Are We Blundering Into Immoral Imperialism?

Historians have long taught that the British blundered into an empire in the eighteenth and nineteenth centuries. In similar fashion, it seems to me, we blundered into imperial action outside the American hemisphere.

For decades we adhered to a foreign policy that had been rationally conceived, consistently followed, and reluctantly accepted by the other great powers. This, of course, was the Monroe Doctrine, which declared that this hemisphere was closed to aggressive action by outside powers and promised that we would not interfere in affairs outside the Americas. This was a unilateral declaration which the other American nations both appreciated and resented.

Franklin D. Roosevelt and Cordell Hull wisely agreed that the Monroe Doctrine should be enforced by collective action of all the American states rather than by us alone. In Asia, however, we have been acting unilaterally rather than collectively through the UN or with other interested powers. It is not enough to say that we are in Southeast Asia to prevent the spread of Communism, because this is hardly the way to accomplish this worthy aim. We blundered into the Pacific before anyone took Communism seriously, and now we are groping to formulate a rational policy about our role outside the American hemisphere.

Perhaps a few reflections on the white man's role in the Asian world might serve as background for formulating a more rational and moral foreign policy in that area. The Chinese had a more highly developed civilization than did Europeans in early medieval times, and they considered white men semibarbaric.

For a time it seemed that missionaries who were willing to adapt to Chinese customs might pioneer in establishing friendly relations with the Chinese. But Rome blundered in condemning the Chinese rites, an action which the Chinese considered insulting to themselves, and the few "civilized" westerners like Father Matteo Ricci. Thereafter the Chinese government tried to isolate itself and its culture from foreign invaders.

The next contacts of any importance came in the nineteenth century when European nations — and later the United States — entered the imperialist race for sources of raw materials, potential markets, areas for capital investment, and places of strategic importance. By mutual agreement the great powers divided the practically defenseless nations, such as China, into "spheres of influence" and eventually "protectorates."

Europeans enjoyed such arms and industrial superiority that the Chinese, Indians, and other "backward" peoples could be subdued and controlled by a handful of men. But they, in turn, took on Western ideas of self-government and national independence. They also took on Western industrial and military techniques.

As a result, hundreds and thousands of men are required to police an area that a handful of English or French soldiers could control a century ago. It is estimated, for example, that it takes $327,000 to kill a single Vietcong.

We were caught up in the imperialist fever in the Spanish American War, after which we annexed Hawaii — where we already had virtual control — as well as the Philippines. President McKinley expressed our new policy in the Pacific with remarkable candor: "The truth is, I didn't want the Philippines, and when they came to us, as a gift from the gods, I did not know what to do with them. . . . And one night late it came to me this way: (1) That we could not give them back to Spain — that would be cowardly and dishonorable; (2) that we could not turn them over to France or Germany — that would be bad business and discreditable; (3) that we could not leave them to themselves — they were unfit for self-government; and (4) that there was nothing left for us to do but to take them all, and to educate the Filipinos, and uplift and civilize and Christianize[!] them, and, by God's grace, do the very best we could by them, as our fellowmen for whom Christ also died. And then I went to bed, and went to sleep and slept soundly."

Thus we blundered into our Asian policy, much as the British had done a century earlier. Now the British have withdrawn, and the question is whether we are going to try to establish a Pax Americana to replace the former Pax Britannica. The British found that putting out brush fires throughout the world overtaxed their resources and earned them worldwide hostility. We are already finding that this is even truer of us.

It is inevitable that we eventually pull out of Vietnam and the rest of Southeast Asia, as we pulled out of the Philippines, as Britain and France and Holland pulled out of their former imperialist areas. This has been the pattern of the rise and decline of imperialism, and there is no reason to believe that it will differ now. But each added commitment, each bomb dropped, each escalation makes the resolution of this problem more difficult.

If the conclusion is that, for both practical and moral reasons, we must eventually return to our former and sounder foreign policy — as I believe it is — then we must focus now on the most expeditious way to terminate our involvement in an area where we have no legitimate business.

If we are true to declarations of principle consistently made since 1945, then we must give up unilateral action outside the American hemisphere in favor of collective action through the UN or the countries affected by our action. Any unilateral action is bound to be considered intolerable by other countries and immoral by most Americans.

5. U. S. Feels Frustrated by Vietnam

Continued escalation of the war in Vietnam, combined with the admission that no permanent gains have been made in bombing missions and the ineffectiveness of both the search-and-destroy strategy and the pacification program, has produced a feeling of weary frustration in this country.

This has caused some former hawks to favor negotiations now, but it has also driven others to demand further and extensive escalation. This latter group argues that the restrictions put on the military in Vietnam explain why the war has dragged out so long. The former group, growing in number and including more and more prestigious persons, argues that further escalation will not secure victory and peace, that even if it would succeed the price would be too high, and that each step of escalation is a step toward a general and a total war.

An irrational but not irrelevant note about our involvement in Vietnam is the issue implicitly suggested by former Premier Ky. What are we fighting for in Vietnam? Are we sincerely fighting for government of the people's choice if we do not allow the Vietcong to have a voice either in the elections or in the peace negotiations? Are we honestly fighting for anything, or only against the specter of Communism? If it is only Communism, have we inquired whether the Vietcong are truly Communists or radical nationalists who believe in self-determination? (This does not in any way condone their terroristic methods, which compare quite unfavorably with methods used by interventionists from another continent.)

The Vietnamese question is not simply academic. Those who

want to escalate the conflict are obliged to show how escalation can bring victory without involving China and perhaps the USSR in a total war. Otherwise victory is suicide. In the light of the failures of past escalations to terminate the conflict, those who favor it have a difficult case to prove. Those who favor termination of the conflict by de-escalation must show ways and means of ending the conflict so as not to leave those we have been supporting at the mercy of their opponents and of withdrawing in such fashion as to leave the self-government we prize a possibility.

Whether to de-escalate and ultimately to withdraw from Vietnam is a political question to be settled in Washington. The most feasible way to do it is a practical question to be settled in consultation with the military, both in the Pentagon and in the field, for this question involves security as well as money and the deployment of our manpower.

Most congressmen and others concerned with ending the war in Vietnam propose to halt the bombing of targets in North Vietnam in the hope that this will be the first step toward negotiations. They do not propose any further plan for de-escalation. General Gavin proposed over two years ago that the United States restrict itself to holding strongly armed enclaves in South Vietnam. This plan would keep us in Vietnam at a minimum cost in money and American lives. It abjures total victory, which Gavin and many others believe is impossible, short of using the big nuclear weapons.

A modification of the Gavin plan was recently proposed by John Kenneth Galbraith, chairman of Americans for Democratic Action. Galbraith suggests that we stop the bombings in the North, retire to military enclaves that can be held at little cost, and provide "the maximum of security, tranquillity and well-being in the limited but populous areas that we control." He also proposes that we "disengage ourselves from the political generals to whom we have become committed in Saigon." This means abandoning the unsuccessful search-and-destroy operation in the sparsely settled rural areas and shifting the ratio of losses more heavily against the Vietcong and North Vietnamese if they should try to drive us from the military enclaves or take over the population centers we control.

Eight Republican congressmen have offered another detailed plan for de-escalation toward an eventual armistice. The plan calls for us to take the initiative by calling a 60-day halt to bombing north of the 21st parallel, which runs between Haiphong and Hanoi. If North Vietnam responded by an equivalent act of de-escalation, we should take the next step of moving the no-bombing line further southward, and so on.

The spokesman for these congressmen, Representative F. Bradford Morse of Massachusetts, explained: "By halting the bombing in stages, by starting the cessation in northern Vietnam and gradually working southward, and by tying each successive stage to equivalent North Vietnamese reductions in its support operations to the south, the plan minimizes the military risks to the United States. The plan calls for a series of small steps, each of which builds confidence in the genuine sincerity of each of the combatants."

The defenders of this plan believe it might work because it does not require simultaneous steps by two governments which do not trust each other, it does not require semi-public negotiations where both sides must think of saving face, it does not deal in ultimatums, and it provides a method of de-escalation by small steps that would be verifiable.

Any plan of de-escalation must presume that Hanoi will respond. No one knows whether they will. There is evidence, however, that there is presently division of opinion in Hanoi's government. There is also the certainty that China is at least temporarily distracted by its own problems and the Soviet Union would be happy to see an end to the war in Vietnam as long as Hanoi does not have to capitulate.

One can only guess at the likelihood of Hanoi responding to initiatives from Washington, but when nothing substantial would be lost from taking the initiative it seems it should be taken because so many lives are at stake and continuation of this war is poisoning our thought on domestic as well as foreign policy.

6. *Thoughts About our Asian Policy*

Every nation must continually reappraise its foreign policy. Otherwise it can be trapped into following a policy as obsolete as France's Maginot Line in 1939 — excellent for World War I, but not World War II. We seem to have been forced by De Gaulle to think of reformulating our policy in Europe, but there is little or no indication that we are doing a basic review of our policy in Southeast Asia. The blustering front put on by Communist China seems to have practically precluded the rational thinking about alternatives and consequences there which are essential for formulating a sound policy.

Some serious questions have to be considered anew, and the old answers have to be studied to see if they are still valid — if they ever were. Why did we commit ourselves to intervention in Southeast Asia? Was the reason valid, and the cause sufficient? Did we understand the consequences of our original commitment? Was it a necessary, a sound, a moral commitment? Have we followed up the original commitment morally? Has the escalation of the conflict in South Vietnam been necessary? Has the public, who must foot the bill in lives and money, been honestly informed of developments in the conflict? Are we going to follow the same pattern of escalation elsewhere, as we are already starting to do in Thailand? If we have conducted our foreign policy soundly in Southeast Asia, why have even the friendly nations of the world — except in the Pacific area — been so critical of our policy? Is a policy — whether right or wrong — implemented morally when direction and timing (involving lives) are done with votes in mind? Can a policy be sound or moral, except by accident, if it is aimed at keeping a consensus happy?

These are not easy questions to answer, but they must be thought through carefully to arrive at as sound and honest a set of answers as possible. As a prelude to arriving at such answers, there are some cold facts that cannot be ignored.

First, Communist China is the most populous nation in the world. It consists of 700 million people, as compared to India's 475 million, the Soviet Union's 230 million, and our 200 million. Nationalist China has but 12.5 million, and Israel only 2.6 million. It is therefore absurd to talk about stable peace in Asia without acquiescence by Red China. Some form of coexistence must be worked out, as it has been with the Soviet Union. The best that can be achieved without including China in eventual negotiations is an armed truce, and this would constitute a continual drain on our financial and human resources which is difficult to defend.

The second fact is that China is badly split on whether to follow Mao's intransigent policy or to take steps toward some kind of accommodation with the rest of the world. Continuation of our present policy helps the intransigents and makes more difficult the work of accommodationists. The terrible irony about fighting Communism, which most Americans refuse to face, is that fighting it and bombing its adherents makes them grow stronger in spirit and more rigid in their "holy war," whereas feeding and clothing it kills it. For then Communists have something to lose and they think much more soberly about a general war. A purely Machiavellian approach dictates forgetting about ideology and concentrating on reality. This coincides with the approach toward all humanity advocated by Pope John XXIII for reasons far from Machiavellian.

The third fact is that Communist China's absence from the United Nations cripples that organization badly, as does our refusal to negotiate through UN Secretary U Thant, who has been thwarted by us in his relaying Hanoi's apparent willingness to consider negotiations. China's absence from the United Nations is a main cause of stalemates on the underground test ban and peacekeeping proposals. There are 121 sovereign nations represented at the UN, several of them with a population less than that of several major U. S. cities. China has a population greater than the total of more than 100 nations at the UN, and still we exclude it when global decisions are considered.

The fourth fact is that Red China does not want to join the United Nations, except on its own terms — which are indicative of its either playing "hard to get" or being trapped by ideology, which will be its undoing. At any rate, it is obvious that we cannot accept China's conditions for admission to the UN, for this would be as unreal as our present policy. The fact is that there are two Chinas, and any realistic policy must be based on this fact. It is also a fact that Nationalist China is as intransigent in its unrealistic stand as Red China is.

The obvious solution toward which we must work is for both Chinas to be in the United Nations, not on the terms demanded by either but on the realistic terms that both of them exist, both of them represent sizeable numbers of people, and both should be heard if the United Nations can expect to deal effectively with problems in Asia. Our long opposition to the admission of Red China on any terms, apparently ending now, has been based on outmoded ideological considerations. If China is unfit for membership according to norms laid down by the UN charter (as I think it is), then we had better think of expelling many other nations, and perhaps excusing ourselves from membership. At any rate, clearly withdrawing our opposition to Communist China's admittance to the United Nations without expelling Nationalist China would put Red China on the spot and take some of the wind out of Mao's sails at home and abroad.

Suppose that we can morally justify our staying in Southeast Asia indefinitely, which at this point seems doubtful. Then the question remains whether the cost is too high. What is to be accomplished by our remaining in the decades to come, and is it enough to justify cutting back on our domestic war on poverty at home? How many thousands of men can be retrained for jobs, for example, for the cost of one B-52 lost on a mission over North Vietnam? What is accomplished by such a mission? What is accomplished by retraining a given number of men replaced by machines? These are hard questions to answer. But neither hawks nor doves can ignore them if they are truly interested in formulating a sound foreign policy in Southeast Asia instead of jousting with ideological windmills.

7. A Hoped-for Direction in Foreign Policy

Every nation's foreign policy is in need of continual review, reappraisal, and readjustment. Unfortunately, both Republican and Democratic administrations long failed to review the policy set by Secretary of State Dulles, except for questioning the doctrine of massive retaliation, and they refused to credit their critics as responsible and loyal Americans who just might have something worth saying. Fortunately, a serious review of foreign policy seems to be in the making.

The underlying mistake is to ground foreign policy on ideological considerations. It is said now that "ideology is dead." But in foreign relations it never was alive and viable.

Foreign relations ultimately resolve themselves into practical, realistic, and always open-ended relations between two or more states, and any government that leaves the world of reality to become a Don Quixote suffers his fate. The Soviet Union survived and grew strong because it dropped Marxian ideology as a guide to both domestic and foreign policy.

Lenin was hard-headed enough to revert to "capitalistic devices" to rescue Russia from the morass into which he had naïvely plunged her by trying to follow Marxist doctrine. After Stalin's horribly harsh five-year plans failed to usher in a Communist utopia, Soviet leaders again had to revert to practices incompatible with Marxist ideology. In foreign relations, too, Soviet statesmen (while mouthing Marxist slogans) have played the standard game of power politics. Theirs became the old game of imperialism, which confused Americans because we listened to the words of the Comintern and Cominform, and

144

failed to discern the pattern of moves followed by Soviet leaders in the chess game of international politics.

In domestic affairs, Soviet leaders occasionally gave ideology another try, each time setting themselves back in the race to become an affluent society. The most notorious of these instances was to follow the genetic theories of Lysenko instead of Mendel, simply because Lysenko's theories fit in better with Marxist ideology. The result was devastating defeat in the "battle of the wheat" and the humiliating need to import tons of grain from Canada and other "capitalistic" countries. Lysenko was reassigned to teach in high school, and Marxist ideology was ignored in favor of better seed grain.

Ideologies can make monsters out of men and out of nations. The Nazi party, driven demoniacally by its ideology, visited horrible destruction on its fellow Germans and then upon the rest of the world. Nor were the Nazis unique. When the Crusaders captured Jerusalem in 1099 they subjected its inhabitants to a terrible massacre. Raymond, Canon of Puy, observed: "Indeed, it was a just and splendid judgment of God that this place should be filled with the blood of the unbelievers, since it had suffered so long from their blasphemies."

In the post-war world Americans had good reason to fear the Soviet Union, and later China. But the reason to have feared them was not so much their ideology of Communism as their imperialistic ambitions backed by hundreds of millions of followers. The Marxist ideology was used indeed to stimulate their people to untold sacrifice and hardship and to strike terror into the rest of the world.

If it had been taken seriously as a guide in either domestic affairs or foreign policy it would have insured self-defeat. So it has been in the countries of Eastern Europe, which have progressed politically and economically in proportion to the way they have deserted their Communist ideology in practice, though not abandoning its slogans.

Failure to understand that ideology is dead as a determinant of foreign policy caused us to create unnecessary difficulties for countries emerging from the delusion of Communism, as our trying to cut off all trade relations with these countries and prevent them from developing viable economies by adopting some "capitalistic" techniques.

Again, failure to think in real terms of persons being killed, or starved, or rescued (what is more real than "brothers in Christ"?) rather than in labels like "Communist" pushes us toward the edge of justifying any atrocity committed in the name of ideology.

The greatest victory that leaders of rival nations could win over us would be to keep us in the unreal world of ideology in the belief that it is truly real.

Doctrine, of course, possesses its own reality. And it can give inspiration and thrust to political and military action. But it cannot guide it and sustain it — except into the unreal world and to jousting with windmills. Therefore we must distinguish between Communism as a philosophy or secular theology, and as a viable political program.

The writing of Marx and successors like Trotsky remain in the study; the political programs of "Communist" countries that have survived may continue to use the slogans of Communist ideologies, but in practice they have had to repudiate them.

This is not to condone, excuse, or approve of the conduct of these countries. It is only to suggest that our statesmen and their critics not fall into the trap of assessing the conduct of these countries in ideological terms.

Alliances, treaties, spheres of influence should all be considered in the light of our own self-defense and the establishment of peace. It is not easy to know where our perimeter of defense should be drawn for the future, but it does not require much reflection to conclude that it is unrealistic to conduct foreign affairs according to ideological considerations.

Moreover, it puzzles and confuses realistic statesmen in other countries, who cannot understand how a nation of financial and technological wizards can be so naïve in thinking about foreign relations.